REBEL
IN THE
SOUL

REBEL
IN THE
SOUL

AN ANCIENT EGYPTIAN
DIALOGUE BETWEEN A MAN
AND HIS DESTINY

BIKA REED

Inner Traditions International
Rochester, Vermont

Inner Traditions International
One Park Street
Rochester, Vermont 05767
www.InnerTraditions.com

LIBRARY OF CONGRESS CATALOGING-IN-PUBLICATION DATA

Dispute of a man with his soul. English & Egyptian.
    Rebel in the soul : an ancient Egyptian dialogue between a man and
his destiny / [translation and commentary by] Bika Reed.
        p.   cm.
    Originally published.
    ISBN 978-089281-615-0
    1. Mysticism—Egypt.   2. Symbolism.   I. Reed, Bika, 1931–
    II. Title.
PJ1681.B413 1997
299'.31—dc21   97-4969
                                                                CIP

Designed by Ken Garland and Associates

Typeset by Inforum Ltd, Portsmouth and John Swain and Son Ltd, London

Printed and bound in the United States
10 9 8 7 6 5

Table of Contents

Publisher's Preface 7

Acknowledgements 8

Introduction 9

History of the Berlin Papyrus 3024 11

Rebel in the Soul 13

The Rebel 89

The Soul 93

An Offering to the Temples 96

Introduction to the Commentary 105

Commentary 107

The Author's Hieroglyphic Transcript
of the Berlin Papyrus 3024 131

To R.A. Schwaller de Lubicz

Publisher's Preface

No matter which tradition it belongs to, a book based on inner knowledge reveals in one way or another, the hidden structure of causal laws which support our obvious, physical reality. These books give our mind access into a dimension which justifies our aspiration and diminishes our natural fears of the absurd and contradictory aspects of life. *Rebel in the Soul* is such a book.

Contact with R.A. Schwaller de Lubicz was a turning point in the life of the author. Following the way indicated in the work of de Lubicz, Bika Reed dedicated herself to the study of Ancient Egyptian symbolical thought. After working on the hieroglyphic writings, she developed a line of original work in the field of mythological symbolism. Her work is based completely on the reading of original hieroglyphic texts and not on translations.

Rebel in the Soul is the fruition of twenty years of study and research into the essential structures which are at the base of the Egyptian way of thinking. It represents the first coherent and consistent translation of an Ancient Egyptian sacred text, and proves a fully developed philosophical system in Egypt, more than a thousand years before Plato. Translations of the *Bhagavad Gita* and *Tao Te Ching* have brought to us the mystical heritage of the East. *Rebel in the Soul* opens to the West the door to its own origins, Ancient Egypt.

Bika Reed's work represents a step further in rendering accessible to us Ancient Egyptian thought, not as a mere addition to our knowledge, but as a spiritual ferment.

Ehud C. Sperling

Acknowledgements

I wish to express my gratitude:

To Claudine Nemejanski Fischer, for her moral sustenance.

To my husband, Stuart, and my son, Daniel, for their patience.

To Providence, which has put my book in the hands of Ehud Sperling. Thanks to him, I saw, after eleven weeks of my first visit to New York, nothing but his office, the underground, and the flat I was staying in. He acted, while editing my book, like a very old midwife. He knew when to sit quietly, shaking back and forth, whilst I was giving birth to a new phrase. But he also knew when to cross out, with incomparable brutality, some of my best writing ever: Ehud has that rare form of intellect which characterises great producers, he knows how to fight over-expansion, and thus expand clarity, without interfering with the creative work of an author. His utter dedication to this task, regardless of time and available energy, is an effect of a total commitment to this work.

To Ken Garland, for his understanding and generosity.

To Lucie Lamy, for her kindness and long-standing readiness to help me in my work.

Introduction

The nameless, hieratic papyrus 3024, from the Berlin Museum, was translated for the first time in 1896 by the German scholar Adolph Erman. This translation was published along with a hieroglyphic transcript under the name: *Gespräch Eines Lebensmüden mit Seiner Seele (A Man Tired of Life in Dispute with his Soul)*. The beginning of the papyrus is lost. Its origin and date are uncertain.

Some scholars have placed it in the 'Intermediate Period' between the Old and Middle Kingdom (2500-1991 B.C.), others later. The author is unknown. The apparent theme is suicide. For nearly a century, it has presented a challenge to Egyptologists.

Many translations have appeared of this lamentation of *A Man Tired of Life*. All of these interpretations, however, are lacking in consistency. These inconsistencies must be ascribed to the scholars and not to Egypt, a civilization which was built on consistency itself. Long before the theory of relativity, the sages of Egypt knew that our material reality consisted of movement, measure and proportion. But this vision did not produce in Egypt uncertainty and doubt in the natural values of life, for they also perceived a mystical reality underlying the material world. To indicate that reality, they did not make use of abstract symbols, but instead evoked it through the concrete and visible: a hand, a foot, an owl. By the known, the Egyptian hieroglyphs evoked the unknown.

While translating the Berlin Papyrus 3024 and reviewing earlier interpretations, I experienced awe at encountering the most astonishing philosophical language ever conceived by man, and at the same time felt sorrow at witnessing its debasement. It seemed to me that what remains of the original thought in these translations of the Berlin Papyrus could be compared to what would be left of Shakespeare if in many thousands of years, a linguistic archaeologist uncovered a torn fragment of *Hamlet*:

King: Now, Hamlet, where is Polonius?
Hamlet: At supper.
King: At supper? Where?
Hamlet: Not where he eats, but where he is eaten; a certain convocation of politic worms are e'en at him. Your worm is your only emperor for diet; we fat all creatures else to fat us, and we fat ourselves for maggots; your fat king and your lean beggar is but variable service; two dishes, but one table; that's the end.

The archaeologist, using magnifying glasses to read the tattered leaf, would carefully examine the text and compose an article on it for the scientific *Ancient British Excavation Memorial Society*. Entitled, *The Gastronomic Habits of the Ancient British*, the paper would give evidence for the following conclusions:

'The ancient British considered maggots as their main food. It must have been a long extinct variety (maggot comestibus), unknown today. The flesh of the maggot was highly esteemed, for even the king ate it, as indicated in line five. The text, though obscure and corroded, leaves no doubt that social distinctions were clearly demarcated by size: to be fat was both an honor and a social advantage, whilst to be lean was the stigma of beggary and low birth. Eating maggots was so important that all state functions were concluded by this gastronomic event.'

The Berlin Papyrus 3024, along with many of the sacred texts of Egypt, has suffered a similar fate. It is strange that so simple and evocative a language as Ancient Egyptian should be obscured by the very instrument of its rediscovery, the Egyptologist. No matter how academically erudite and analytically brilliant, can somebody who believes that Ancient Egypt was a primitive society, incapable of abstract thought, transmit to the modern reader its wisdom? Like a surgeon, who, searching for the soul of his patient with the help of a scalpel, declares there is no soul in man, the analytical mind, bent over a papyrus, with the scalpel of grammar, cries out, 'there is no philosophy in Egypt!' To such a mentality, the voyage of the Barque of the Sun is merely a pagan dream. Yet *their* objective reality would be a dream to the wise men of Egypt. It is as if a sleepwalker were placed as judge over the awake.

The evolution of consciousness, symbolized by the Barque of the Sun, moving through the Underworld (the unconscious), is the main theme of Ancient Egyptian sacred writings. Stages of this evolution were often treated individually on the walls of tombs and in papyri. In this voyage, at a certain 'hour' (stage), we meet the Rebel in the Soul. I have given this new title to the papyrus because it speaks of that hour of spiritual transformation.

Rebel in the Soul is an initiatic text, dedicated to this critical stage: intellectual rebellion. It was meant for students of the Temple, whose highly developed intellect was approaching this crisis.

Today, in a world where highly developed intellect is at war with basic social and human needs and where, simultaneously, young intuitive forces are searching for a new way, this initiatic text is vital. It draws attention to the typical phenomenon arising from that conflict, and also offers a solution to it. To prepare our minds to assess the nature of this conflict and this solution is the main goal of the papyrus. The intellectual rebel believes that his only real choice in life is suicide. But there is no choice in suicide, only weakness of an intellect unable to understand that there cannot be an alternative to life, only to death. Here the crucial role of intellect in spiritual survival is assessed in its most deeply paradoxical nature.

Egypt often expresses man's inner conflict by the image of the field and the plougher. There is no instant liberation, no other solution to our problems, except cultivation, a balanced development of man's spiritual potential. At the peak of its evolution, like the mature fruit, intellect has to face its inevitable transformation, to be able to perpetuate its seed, life itself.

A History
of the Berlin Papyrus 3024

1843 The German Egyptologist, Richard Lepsius purchases the only existing copy of a nameless hieratic papyrus from the Athanasi Collection, London, and brings it to Berlin.

1859 Lepsius publishes a text of the hieratic papyrus without a translation.

1896 The German Egyptologist, Adolf Erman publishes a hieroglyphic transcript of the text with the first translation, under the title: *Das Gespräch eines Lebensmüden mit seiner Seele (A Man, Tired of Life, in Dispute with his Soul)*. Subsequent translations have retained the title, and made use of the same transcript.

1962 The English Egyptologist, R.J. Williams publishes a review of the published translations.

1969 German Egyptologist, Winfrid Barta publishes a study of the text, taking 37 translations into account. Barta stresses the difficulties posed by the text, calling them unparalleled among all the texts of Egypt.

The Papyrus consists of 155 lines of text, which its first translator, Erman divided into 62 lines of 'poetry' and 93 lines of prose. This division has also been followed by all subsequent translators.

Erman's translation of the 62 lines of 'poetry' is already in a consistent and meaningful form. But the sense of the prose passages has eluded all the translators, who attribute the confusion to the Egyptians. Those passages were treated as 'obscure' mortuary notes.

Translator's Notes

In translating, I used the hieroglyphic text published in JEA, 42, 1956 by R.O. Faulkner.

Lacunae in the text are marked by dots.

Proposed restorations of sections destroyed in the original text are marked by parentheses. Those restorations are only proposed in cases of small lacunae, or faint traces, as they fit in the space and with the sense of the text. Bigger lacunae are left without an attempt of restoration.

The layout of the dialogue is not a part of the original text, as in the Ancient Egyptian language, punctuation was not used.

Illustrations in this book do not belong to the original text. They are conceived as an evocative complement to the dialogue and commentary. The link between the text and this graphic complement is evocative of the basic symbolical concepts underlying the papyrus. It starts by a series of images of the ASS, standing for the Rebel, the man 'tired of life' — and simultaneously for the beast of burden or carrier of his eventual redemption (as we shall see in the commentary, the ass, the most stubborn animal in the world was in Egypt a living symbol of intellectual rebellion).

The majority of illustrations in this book have been reproduced by kind permission of the Library of the Egyptian Museum, Cairo.

We would also like to thank the following organizations and individuals for the illustrations on the pages indicated. The Trustees of the British Museum (66 & 76); Ronald Sheridan Photo Library (14, 70 & 89); Lucy Lamy for her illustrations from *Temple de l'Homme* by R.A. Schwaller de Lubicz (91, 109 & 112); The Louvre, Paris (90); St Marks, Venice (90); General Research and Humanities Division, New York Public Library, Astor, Lenox and Tilden Foundations (91); Kunsthistorisches Museum, Vienna (110 & 123); Bibliotheque Nationale, Paris (112 & 117); Griffin Institute, Ashmolean Museum, Oxford (119); Estate of C.J. Jung, Walter Verlag Olten 172 (122) and The Petrie Museum, University College, London (126).

Rebel in the Soul

. . . .[1]

I spoke to my Soul
I replied to what it had said:

O! Now

this I cannot bear

My Soul replies not

Indeed, worse than anger is this indifference.[2]

Don't go my Soul!

Stay!

Only with me will you arise![3]

. . . .

. . . .

[If I do not enmesh you] in my body

as the cord within the net,

through no fault of yours will you be lost

[on the Day of Trial.][4]

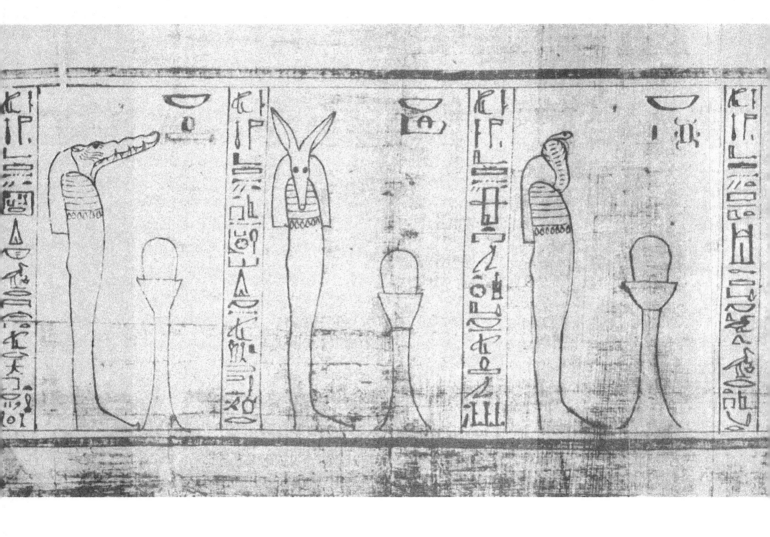

They will judge my Soul!

For I have gone astray,

For I have not obeyed,

Rushing to die before Death has come,

casting to the flame

that which the Soul sustains.[5]

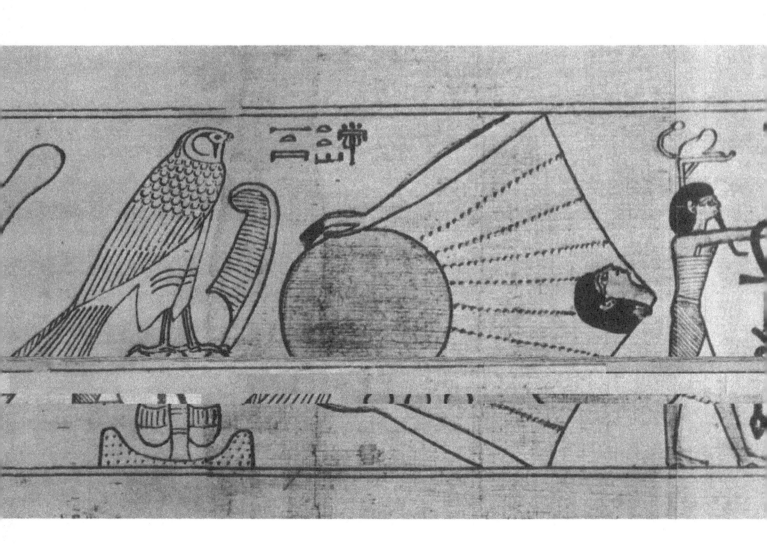

. . . .

Penetrate me

on that Day of Trial!

You will stand up on the Other Side,

enacting the miracle

of the Creator.

Such is his nature:

He comes forth by extracting

himself

from himself.[6]

It is mad, o Soul:

You endure the pain of Life,
    denying me Death
    until death has come!

To enjoy through me the Beyond:
    would that be worse?

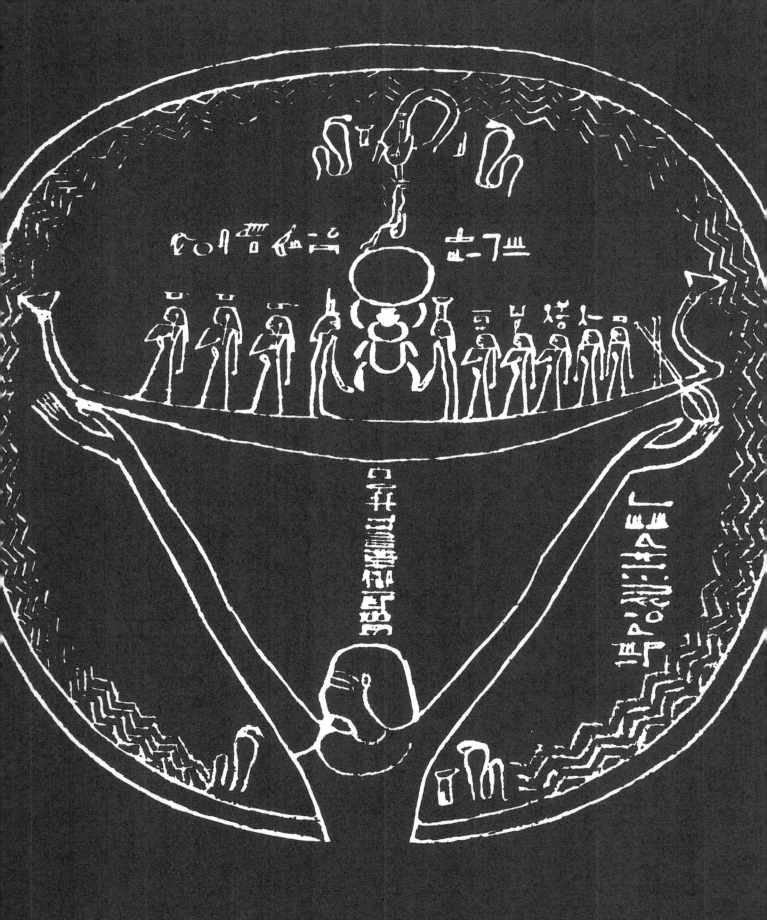

See! Life is but

movement of

Eternal
Return

Even trees fall.[7]

Trample upon evil! Appease my pain!

Let

Djehuti

judge me: He who holds the balance
of natural law.

Khonsu

will defend me: Scribe of the Truth
Above the Law.

Ra

will heed my words: He guides
the Holy Barque of Night.

Isdes

will absolve me
in the Hall of Judgement where I am.

Unhappy me,

crushed beneath the [weight of my heart]
which He will raise up
in the Mystical Encounter
with the

Lord of Transformations

hidden in my body.[8]

The reply of my soul:

What kind of man are you?

Have you lived out your life to its conclusion?

You fret over life like the Lord of Heaps

I have spoken!

I take no part in it!

Nefa is already

one foot off the ground.[9]

If you do not take care

Any evil could possess you.

You will be brought to a stop.

Your name will die![10]

Only through the living Nefa

Can intellect reach the heart,

and Beyond become

the Haven

for the upstream struggle.[11]

. . . .

Ah! If I could heed my Soul

I would not impede the union of its heart with me.

Then, by my hand it would arrive
blissful

      at the Beyond,

like the One within his Pyramid
who stood up, Survivor of his own Burial[12]

BUT in this body, which is yours,

I am the progeny of the Great Ass Iai!

In you I call forth the Other

O Soul unawakened!

I am the progeny of Iai,

A fire which will never cool

I cause the Other to burst forth

O Soul in Flame!

I consume the True Source

In sustaining the Shadow.

I wake the Other,

hungry for torment.

Deeper than Death I destroy the Soul in its husk.

Thus you will never arrive.[13]

Endure, my Soul!
Assist in the creation
of my Divine Heir.

He will present the Offering
Rising from the tomb
On the day of Burial

Putre   factio.

He will install Himself in Everlastingness.[14]

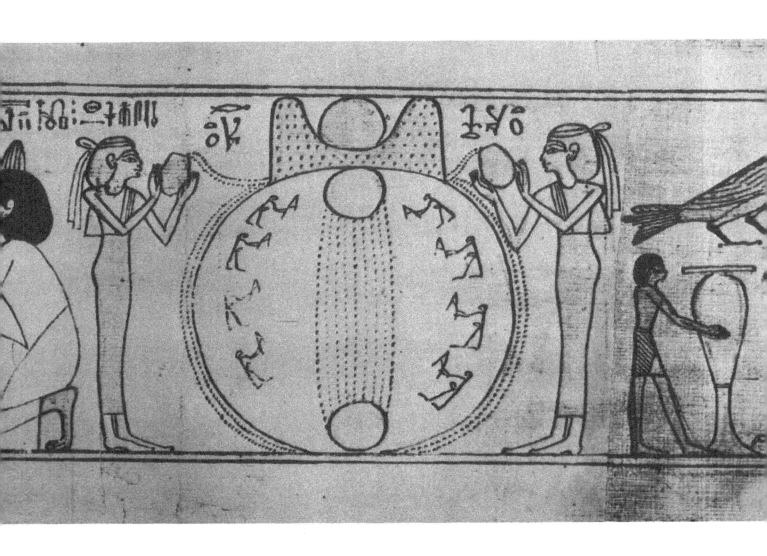

My Soul spoke to me in reply to what I had said:

Remember!

Such a burial is a sorry matter!
Tears flow!
The lost man is cast from his house
and flung upon the Hill!
You shall never reach that summit
to gaze upon the rising and setting Sun.

Even those who shaped granite
To perpetuate in the Pyramid
Virtues of Creation,
builders like Gods:

Their sceptres fell to dust
as on the riverbank, the Unawakened
who lies dead, without Heir;

The flood takes him
The sun takes him
Fish talk to him
In shallow water.[15]

47

Listen to me

See, it is good for man to understand

How to follow the day and overcome despair!

A man did plough his plot.

He did load his harvest onto a barge;

             he towed it along.

His triumphal day was approaching.

He saw the storm gathering from the north.

He kept vigil in the boat.

But the sun went down!

In the dark,

on the Lake of the Crocodile

calamity struck:

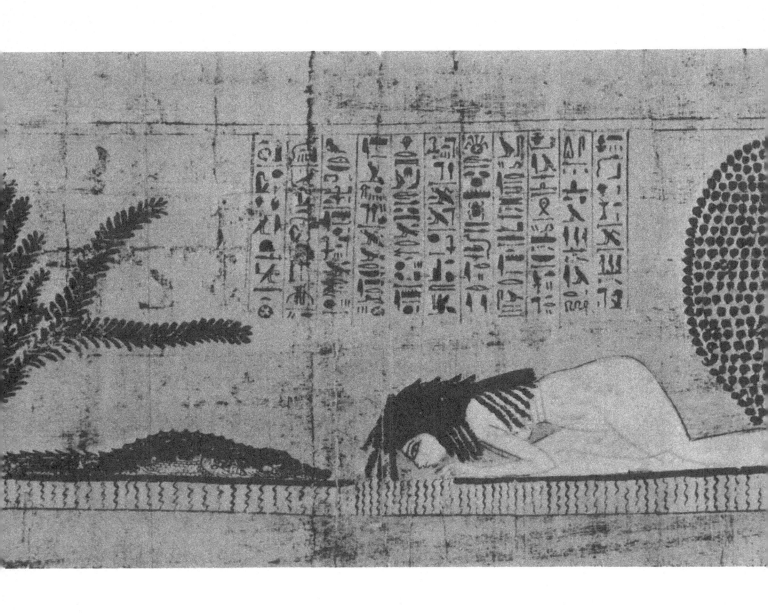

His wife, his children fell to the crocodiles

When it was all over,

after he had regained his voice,

he concluded:

For she who bears children

for she who will never, ever return

from Beyond as a woman again

I do not weep.

I grieve for her children

crushed in the egg,

who looked into the face of the Double Crocodile

before they had lived![16]

A man demanded his Evening Meal.

His wife replied: it is on its way.

He stalked out in rage.

And when, at last, he came home,

he was no longer himself.

His wife spoke to him wisely:

how in his rage he did not recognize

the barren hearts of those who presume.[17]

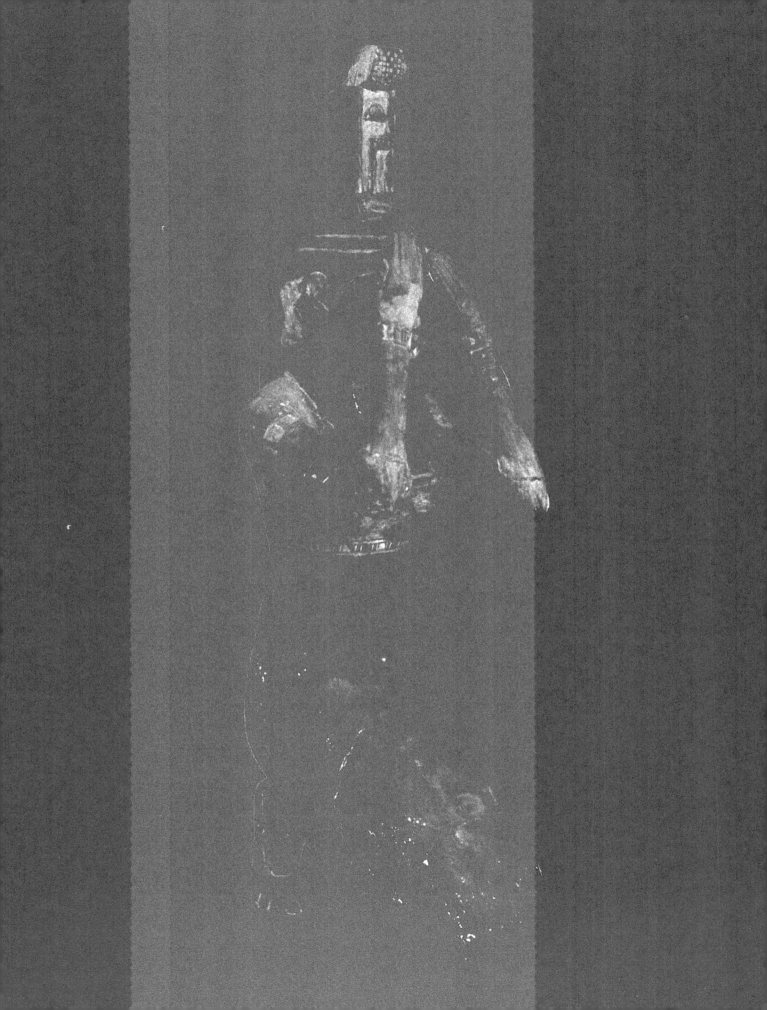

I spoke to my Soul
in reply to what it had said:

Aye! Loathsome is my name!

Aye! Worse than the stench of carrion under the burning skies

of a summer's day!

Aye! Loathsome is my name!

Aye! Worse than fish rejected from the catch!

Rotting under the burning sky!

Aye! Loathsome is my name!

Aye! Worse than the stink of brooding ducks

nesting among the reeds!

Aye! Loathsome is my name!

Aye! More than the smell of fishermen!

More than the creeks of the marshes

where they have fished!

Aye! Loathsome is my name!

Aye! Worse than the smell of crocodile!

Worse than sitting on the muddy shores

        where the crocodiles breed!

Aye! Loathsome is my name!

Aye! Worse than a woman

        who tells lies to her man!

Aye! Loathsome is my name!

Aye! Worse than a strong youth

        showing weakness before his rival!

Aye! Loathsome is my name!

Aye! It is a closed circle around the captured renegade,

        aware of his own end.

To whom shall I speak today?
Brothers are evil.

            Friends, today, cannot be loved.

        To whom shall I speak today?
Rapacious are hearts!

            Each man takes his neighbor's goods.

        [To whom shall I speak today?]
Gentleness is overthrown

            Violence rules all.

        To whom shall I speak today?
When dishonor goes unremarked,

            honor is debased.

To whom shall I speak today?

        He, whose villainy outrages the decent

is acclaimed by the mob for his evil deed.

To whom shall I speak today?

        Men are pirates.

Each man seizes his neighbor's goods.

To whom shall I speak today?

        When vice is greeted as a friend,

the brother who will remonstrate becomes a foe.

To whom shall I speak today?

        Forgotten is the past.

Good deeds go unreturned.

To whom shall I speak today?

The brethren are wicked.

One goes to the barbarian to find righteousness.

To whom shall I speak today?

Disfigured are the faces!

Each man avoids facing his brothers.

To whom shall I speak today?

Hearts are rapacious.

There is not a heart for a man to put his trust in.

To whom shall I speak today?

Gone are the just!

The land is given over to iniquity.

To whom shall I speak today?

        There are no trustworthy friends.

One is pushed into darkness before one can cry out!

To whom shall I speak today?

        The Serene Heart is gone;

and He who follows him is no more.

To whom shall I speak today?

        I am crushed with grief

from loss of He Who Enters the Heart.

To

whom

shall I

speak today?

For corruption

roams the Earth:

there is no end to it!

To die, to me, today

is health to the sick:

like deliverance from slavery.

To die, to me, today

is odor of myrrh;

like a shelter from a windy day.

To die, to me, today

is to smell the lotus;

like being on the shore of ecstasy.

To die, to me, today

is the coming Flood;

like returning home from war.

To die, to me, today

is the unveiling of the sky;

like transfiguration by the Unknown.

O, to die, to me, today

is like longing to see home

after years held in bondage.

In truth, He Who Dwells Within

will absolve this Crime
and this Transgressor.

In truth, He Who Dwells Within

will rise in the Holy Barque of Night
to consecrate the Supreme
Offering to the Temples.

In truth, He Who Dwells Within, the Knower,

will not be denied
when he holds Ra
to his word!

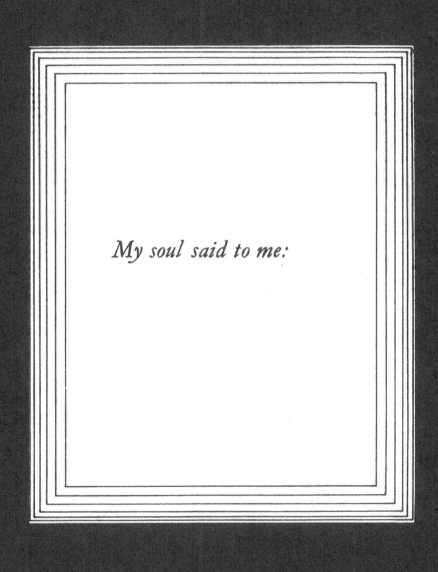

My soul said to me:

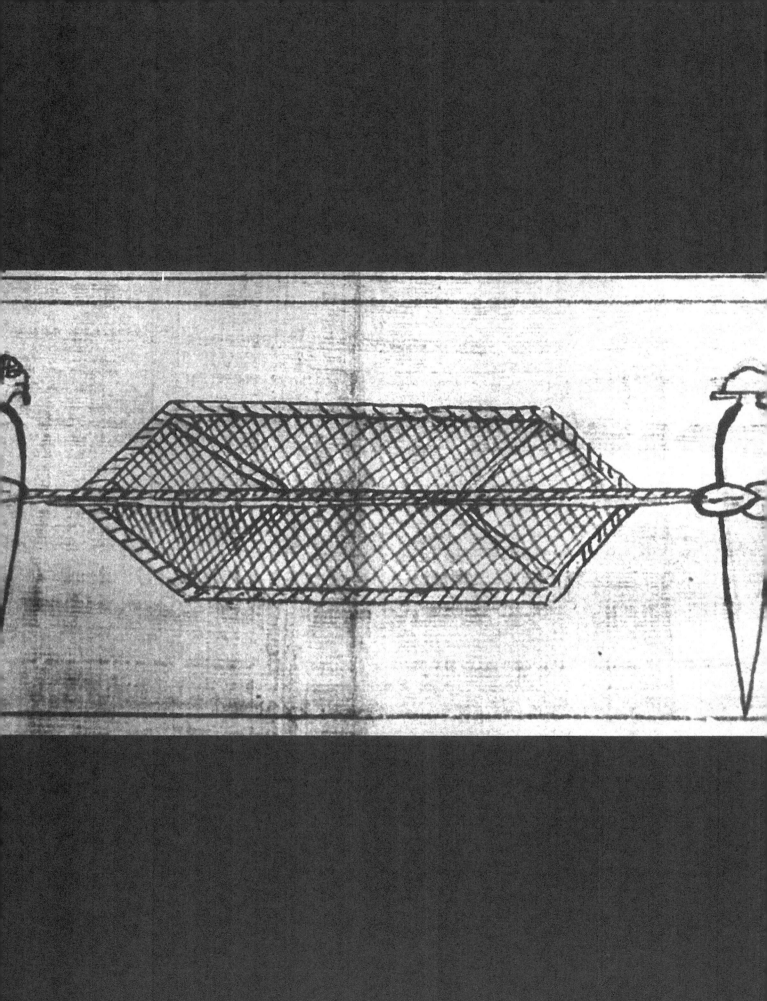

You are hanging up
your misery,

But that Peg,

it belongs to Me!

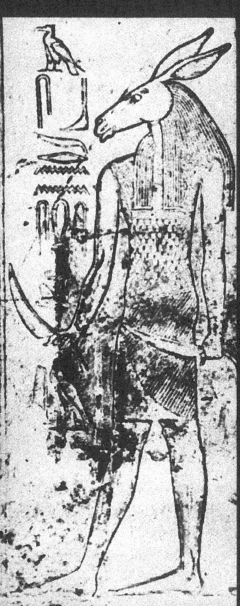

Brother,

 as long as you burn

you belong to life.

You say you want Me with you

in the Beyond?

Forget the Beyond!

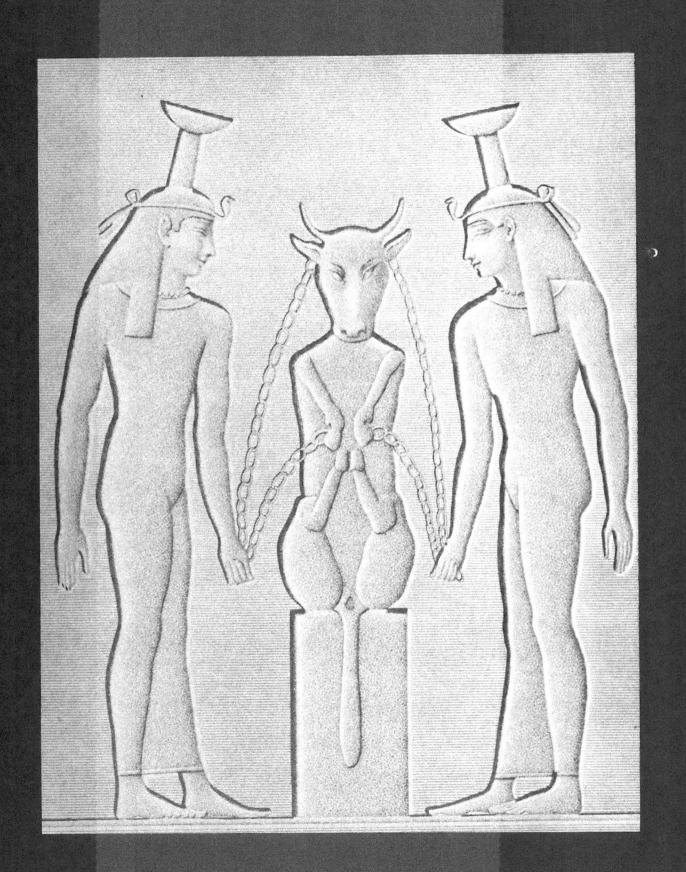

When you bring your flesh to rest
And thus reach the Beyond,

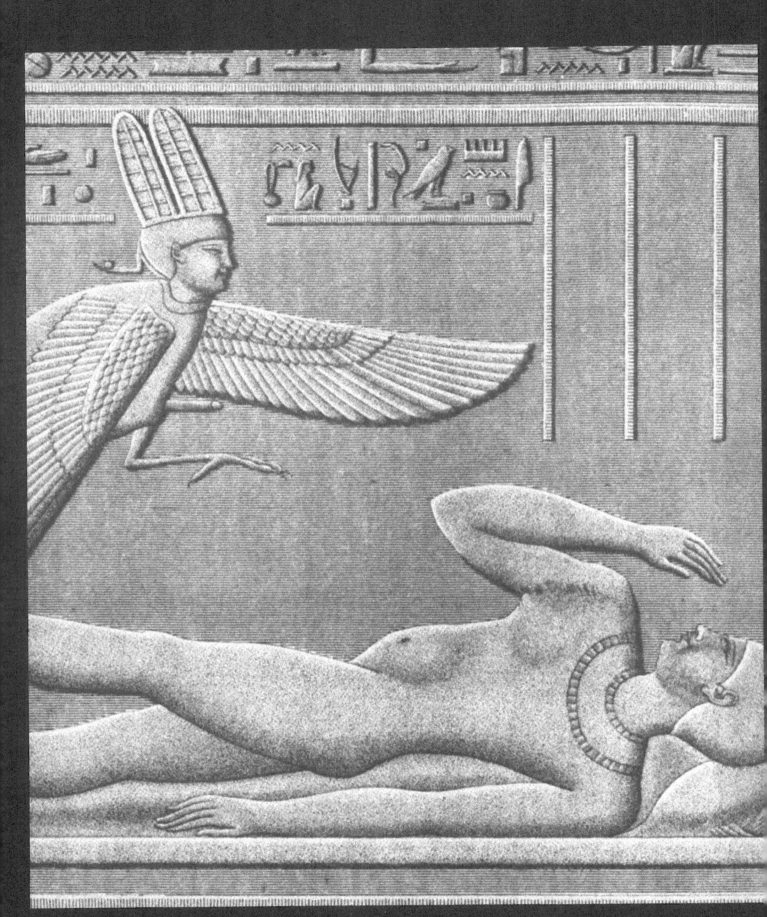

In that stillness

shall I alight upon you;

then united

we shall form the Abode.

for above

is exalted by

below

as is written in the Scriptures.[21]

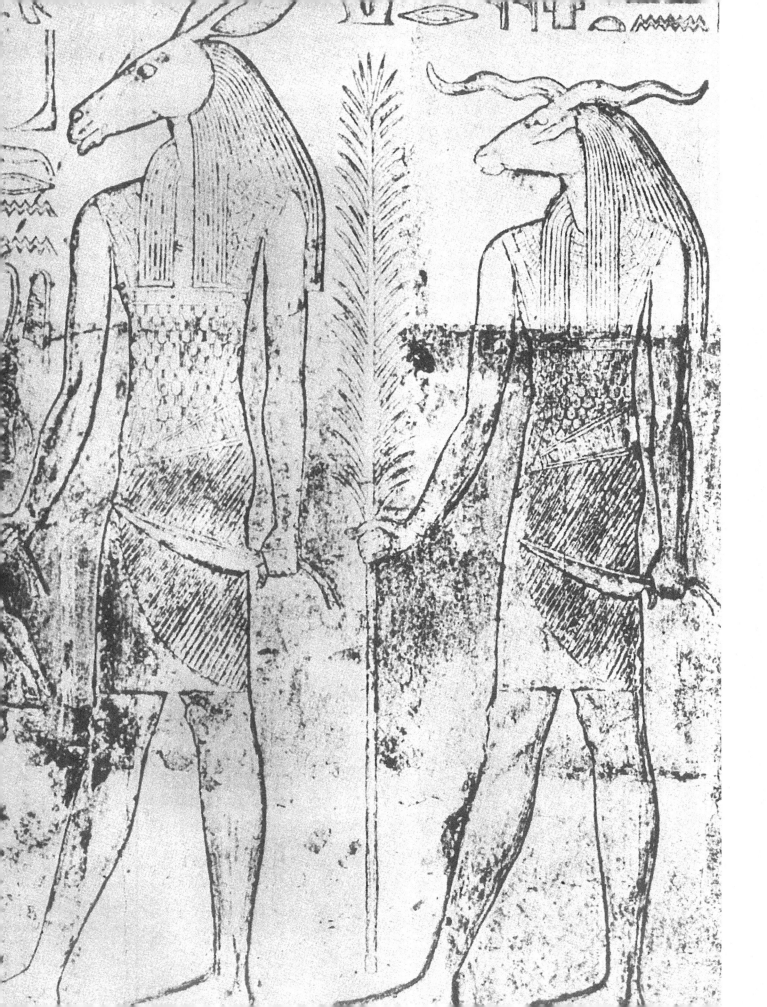

The Rebel

The stubborn, passionate, long-suffering ass is a perfect natural symbol of our rational personality. It bears, like the ass, the weight of all our suffering, and carries us through life. It is stubborn, selfish and refuses 'to go' where we think is best.

Yet, paradoxically, it is the same stubborn 'ass', and only the ass, that can carry the Rebel to salvation; mounted upon the ass, man is mounted upon his own rebellion. The ass is the father of all rebels, but also the carrier of redemption.

IAI, the Great Ass — intellectual rebellion — the Ninth Hour

IAI, the Great Ass, is an aspect of the sun 'god' with ass's ears. We find his image in the *Book of the Gates*, carved on the alabaster sarcophagus of Seti I (fourteenth century B.C.). The *Book of the Gates* depicts the progression of the sun through the night. The twelve hours of the Dark Night are depicted as regions of the Underworld. Each region is an 'hour' of the Night and has its gate. To pass the gate, one has to know the name of its Guardian.

The consciousness moves through the Underworld from gate to gate in a process of slow animation. For Egypt, life and consciousness are synonymous. To be dead meant to be unawakened and inert, moved like a leaf by the wind. 'To be dead', for Egypt, is a state of inanimation, preceding consciousness or life. The process of animation, depicted in the *Book of the Gates* was called *Coming Forth Into Day*. It was also the title of many papyri found in the tombs and was only called *The Book of the Dead Man* by the early tomb robbers. This title was later usurped by Egyptologists and placed upon their publication of a collection of those papyri, entitled *The Book of the Dead*.

The Holy Barque of Night carries the sun through the Underworld (unconsciousness). In this Night, the hours are stages of transformations towards awakening.

IAI is found in the section known as the Ninth Hour. In this Ninth Hour, a crisis menaces the progress of the boat. A double monster, half snake, half crocodile, SHES-SHES, faces the boat.

In the water, between the monster and the boat is IAI, the Great Ass, holding onto a rope which in turn is held by three harpooners. The Ass and the three harpooners precede the Barque of the Sun. Still half immersed in water, IAI clutches the rope. Is he trying to raise himself? Or is he being thrown by the harpooners to the monster? It is hard to tell.

IAI, the bait, clutches the rope which offers him in sacrifice

Opposite: 'He Who Burns' is the name of the herald who opens in us the door to the Beyond

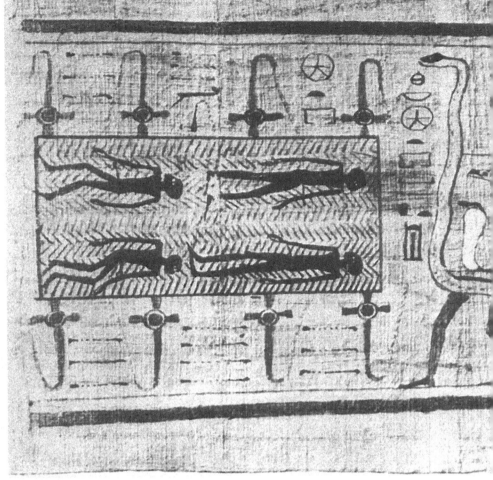

The unawakened in the Lake of Fire

Alchemical Bath

St John in the Fiery Bath

In the preceding scene of the Eighth Hour, we see inert figures immersed in the water: the floating unawakened (NNEW). We find the same image in Medieval alchemy linked to the alchemical bath, or vessel of transformations.

The text of the *Book of the Gates* says: 'We open for thee the hidden place. We make straight for thee the way to Beyond,' proclaiming the same message as John the Baptist. 'Rise up, O ye, Beings of Time, pay ye heed to RA, for it is He who ordered your destinies!' RA responds 'O ye who are immersed in water, ye who are under the water, stretch out your legs, O ye who float, let there be breath for your nostrils, O ye, who are deep in the waters ... ye shall pass through the waters of NU.'

The Eighth Hour holds out the promise of spiritual awakening. The Ninth Hour fulfills this promise with a paradox. The act of awakening is inseparable from the act of rebellion. IAI rises, symbolizing the sun circumscribed by ass's ears. He confronts the Abyss, portrayed as a double monster: His own static, fathomless duality unreconciled. As a double being, sun and ass, IAI is the embodiment of an opposition of forces: a cross. IAI is a cross in human form. The sun is confined between the ears

The 'hook' catching the monster: the figure identified with the hook brandishes the two sceptres (sacrifice and engendering) above the subdued monster

Christ upon the Ass

The Bait

of the rebellious and traditionally recalcitrant 'Ass'. In the gospels, Christ appears mounted on the Ass. It is the Ninth Hour: And about the ninth hour, Jesus called with a loud voice, 'My God, my God, why hast Thou forsaken me!'

IAI is the 'bait' that is offered to the monster, blocking the progress of the sun. But at the same time in a desperate attempt to save himself he clutches a rope which leads him to death. Although offered in sacrifice, he is an integral part of the symbolic complexity that is the Solar Procession. Though the bait, IAI is the forefront of the procession; in a very real sense he leads it. He is the 'hook' that will catch the monster (one of Pharoah's names is the Great Hook). Without the self-sacrifice of IAI, the Barque of the Sun will never traverse the night to the light of dawn. Man will never integrate with his mystical body, or soul.

In our text, the man says: 'In your body I am the progeny of the Great Ass, IAI.' He knows that his despair is the critical tension of spiritual birth. Yet, in his terror, like IAI, he clutches at the rope, that offers him as bait to the double-monster. In this crisis, the rational mind is faced with unknown, rationally inaccessible factors. Thus, in front of destruction, it acts contrary to its salvation and by this 'ignorance' performs unwillingly the sacrifice. It grasps like IAI, the rope of its death. The Rebel must die so that the procession of the Barque of the Sun can continue.

The double-monster

The Soul

The BA of RA and the BA of Osiris united

The ram

Faced with the choice of leaving the Egyptian word BA in the text, or using the classical translation of it, the soul, I have decided to use the word 'soul', although this translation is not entirely satisfactory. The main reason for this choice is simply that I could not find another word which could express, as closely, the all encompassing quality of BA. I also prefer a familiar word like 'soul' in the opening sentences of a text, in itself full of unfamiliar concepts.

BA — Soul — the principle of cohesion or unity

The BA of a living man, evoked in Egyptian myth by the image of a stork still lives in the legend of a baby 'brought by a stork'. In fact, the stork-baby-chimney metaphor expresses the main features of the Egyptian BA. It is the *animating* (birth, baby) and *spiritual* (bird, a volatile spirit) *fire* (chimney). The stork is a migratory bird; this migratory element stands for both reincarnation and transcendance. (The latter is symbolized by the BENU bird or phoenix).

Today, this childish legend is of little value in understanding the complexity of the BA. The BA takes many forms: a stork, a stork with human head, a falcon with human head, a ram, or a human figure with a ram's head. It is also identified with NUT, the soul of the world. Basically a symbol of cohesion, BA represents the unity which mystically links the apparent oppositions of life. Every living phenomenon has its own BA. In man, all aspects of BA are present. His individual personality has its own BA, or 'stork'. This 'stork' is an individual expression of the BA of Osiris, and is doomed, like all individuality, to suffering, death and migration from life to life. Simultaneously, the BA of RA also lives in man, a falcon with a human head. When a man reaches wisdom, the BA of Osiris unifies itself with the BA of RA. This act of union is symbolized by the BENU bird (phoenix).

Opposite: the Soul

NUT, the sky, is the soul of the world

We could say, using a natural image, that the BA, the animating spiritual base of life, could be visualized as an egg. Like the BA, the egg can be assessed in a multi-dimensional way. It is a *totality, potentiality, matrix* and also a synthesis of evolution, the image of *genesis*. We could, in fact, reproduce a total, consistent philosophical network, starting and finishing with an egg.

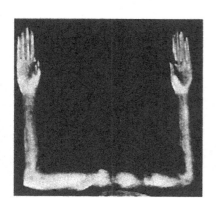

The glyph of KA shows two arms raised

In the yolk, the chick wakes to life, and by growing, devours the egg. Apparently, the egg is doomed to 'sacrifice'. But the same process can be understood in the opposite way: BA is the spiritual, life-sustaining matrix, undetermined and androgynous. This matrix sustains its own determined (polarized) essence, which could be compared to individuality, and was called the KA in Egypt. The BA envelops and sustains its KA, which is its own potential. The chick itself is a new unity; the 'heir', and exaltation of the egg. Like the chick, the KA, or soul's magnetic essence, absorbs the egg and rises as its 'heir', thus giving birth to himself by 'extracting himself from himself'. Therefore, though the outward, physical aspect of the egg appears as restriction, a prison, its underlying purpose and goal is freedom.

In the text of this papyrus, the intellectual rebel argues that suicide is a means of instant liberation. But the man has not yet achieved unity within himself. If the egg is smashed before the chick has formed, a still-birth takes place; there is no liberation. It is only a kind of nuclear explosion, a release of wild 'energy': the loss of Soul.

Egypt teaches us to see our individuality as a whole 'egg': to simultaneously view our inner duality and our hidden potential. In this papyrus, the man haunted by the vision of the absurd contradiction and conflict inherent in life, is met by the teaching of the Temple in the voice of his own BA.

The real obstacle in understanding the ancient Egyptian symbolism is not the ignorance of a secret 'code', but the limited use of our own intel-

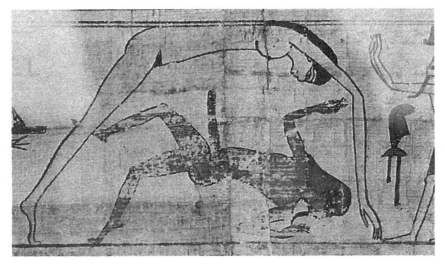

Like GEB (earth), man conceives himself in his soul (sky)

lect. The Egyptian symbolism is in itself an initiation into a more subtle use of intellect. Protected by the unalterable glyph, Egyptian wisdom is still accessible to us in its pure form. It indicates the simultaneous presence in the world and in human beings of both inner conflict and the unity within which it operates, the BA.

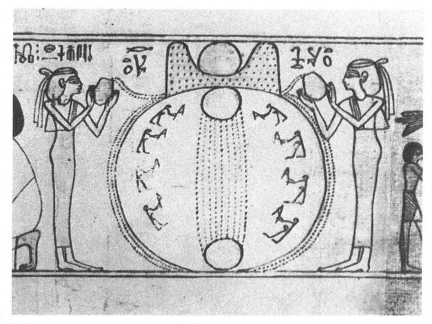

Cycles of birth and death towards the creation of a new indestructable form of life

An Offering
to the Temples

The offering table

In our desire to understand the wisdom of Egypt, we tend to draw Egypt into the sphere of our modern mentality. But our effort will bear no fruit unless we pierce that sphere and try to draw nearer to Egypt.

The difference between those two attitudes can be assessed from the following excerpts of translations of the Berlin Papyrus 3024. On the left, is the work of the distinguished British Egyptologist, R.O. Faulkner and on the right, the dialogue as it appears in this book.

Lines 34f.

'I said: I have not gone,
(even though) that is on the
ground. Indeed thou leapest
away(?), but thou wilt not
be cared for. Every
prisoner says: 'I will take
thee', but thou art dead
though thy name lives.
Yonder is a resting
place attractive(?)
to the heart; the West is
a dwelling place rowing . . . .
. . . face. If my guiltless soul
listens to me and its heart
is in accord with me, it will
be fortunate, for I will
cause it to attain the West,

I take no part in it!
NEFA is already one foot off
the ground.
If you do not take care
Any evil could
possess you.
You will be brought to a stop.
Your name will die!
Only through the living NEFA
can intellect reach the heart,
and Beyond become the Haven
for the upstream struggle . . .
Ah! If I could heed my Soul
I would not impede the union
of its heart with me.
Then, by my hand, it would arrive
blissful at the Beyond,

like one who is in his
pyramid, to whose burial a
survivor attended. I will ...
(over?) thy corpse, so that thou
makest another soul
envious(?)

in weariness (?) I will ...
... then wilt thou not be cold,
so that thou makest envious(?)
another soul which is hot.
I will drink water at the eddy,
I will raise up shade(?) so
that thou makest envious(?)
another soul which is hungry.
If thou holdest me back
from death in that manner,
thou wilt not find nowhere
thou canst rest in the West
Be so kind, my soul, my
brother, as to become my heir
who shall make offering and
stand at the tomb on the day
of burial, that he may prepare (?)
a bier for the necropolis.

like the One within his
Pyramid who stood up,
survivor of his own burial.
But in this body, which is yours,
I am the progeny of the
Great Ass IAI!
In you I call forth
the Other O Soul unawakened!
I am the progeny of IAI,
A fire which will never cool
I cause the Other to burst forth
O Soul in Flame!
I consume the True Source
In sustaining the Shadow.
I wake the Other,
hungry for torment.
Deeper than Death
I destroy the Soul in its husk.
Thus you will never arrive.
Endure, my Soul!
Assist in the creation
of my Divine Heir.
He will present the Offering
Rising from the tomb
On the day of Burial
He will install himself
in Everlastingness.

Lines 148f.

What my soul said to me:
Cast complaint upon the peg(?)

my comrade and brother
make offering on the brazier
and cleave to life according
as I have said. Desire me

here,   , thrust thou aside
the West, but desire that thou
mayest attain the West when
thy body goes to earth, so
that I may
alight after thou art dead;
then will we make
an abode together
IT IS FINISHED FROM ITS BEG-
INING TO ITS END JUST AS
IT WAS FOUND IN WRITING

My Soul said to me:
You are hanging up
your misery. But that Peg,
it belongs to Me!
Brother, as long
as you burn
you belong to life.
You say, you want Me
with You in the Beyond?
Forget the Beyond!
When
You put your flesh to rest
and thus reach the Beyond,
in that stillness shall I alight
upon you;
then united
we shall form the Abode.
For Above is exalted by Below
As is written in the Scriptures.

Different as the two passages appear in translation, both are based upon
and adhere to meanings commonly accepted for the individual hieroglyphs. The center column of the table below shows the hieroglyphs for

lines 43-50 in the order in which they appear in the papyrus, with a selection of meanings attributed to the hieroglyphs by the dictionaries. To the left are the meanings chosen by R.O. Faulkner and to the right, those chosen for this translation.

Faulkner		Dictionary		Reed
—		iu	= it is, is	am
I		Y	= I, me, mine	I
will		R	= *a preposition*	
		yr	*futurity, condition*	progeny
...(?)		t	= engendered by	
		n		
note: the meaning of 'NIAI' is unknown		I		
		A	= IAI (*a form of sun-god with the ears of an ass; primordial engenderer in the belly of the ONE*)	the Great Ass
		I		
over	*lacuna*	M	= in	in
		H		
corpse		A	= entrails, corpses, bodies	body
		Tu		
		(*plurality*)		

98

Faulkner	Dictionary			Reed
thy	K	= you, yours		your
makest envious (?)	S DJ D M	} = entice, cause eruption		cause
thou	K	= you, your	}	the other
another	KY	= another		
soul	Ba	= soul		Soul
in	M	= in	}	unawakened
weariness (?)	NNIU	= inertness, weariness, of dead		

Faulkner	Dictionary		Reed
—	iu	= it is, is	am
I	Y	= I, me	I
will	R	= *a preposition*	
	IR		
	T	= engendered by	the progeny
	N		
… (?)	IAI	= IAI (*sun-god with the ears of an ass*)	IAI
	T		
wilt not	M	= *negative verb*	will not
thou *note: the third person yields but poor sense*	F	= he, his	he
	H		
be cold	S	= to cool, be cold	cool
	U		
	S		
	DJD		
makest envious (?)	M	= entice, cause eruption	wake

Faulkner		Dictionary		Reed
		K	= you, yours	
another		KY	= another	the other
soul		Ba	= Soul	Soul
which		NTY	= which	
is hot *note: the benefits here described are a little obscure, but apparently, mean that if the soul is good it will neither freeze nor fry*		TA	= hot, temper, flame	flame
drink		S UR R	= to drink	consume
I		I		
I		I	= I	I

Faulkner		Dictionary		Reed
water		MW	= water, semen	
at		HR	= upon	
				true source
the eddy		BABAT	= inshore eddy? flowing stream, swirl, inner source?	
raise up		TSY	= set up, raise, support	sustaining
I will		Y	= I, me	
shade (?)		SHUT	= shadow	the shadow
makest envious (?)		SDJDM	= entice, cause eruption	wake
thou		K	= you, your	the other
another		KY	= another	
soul		Ba	= Soul	Soul

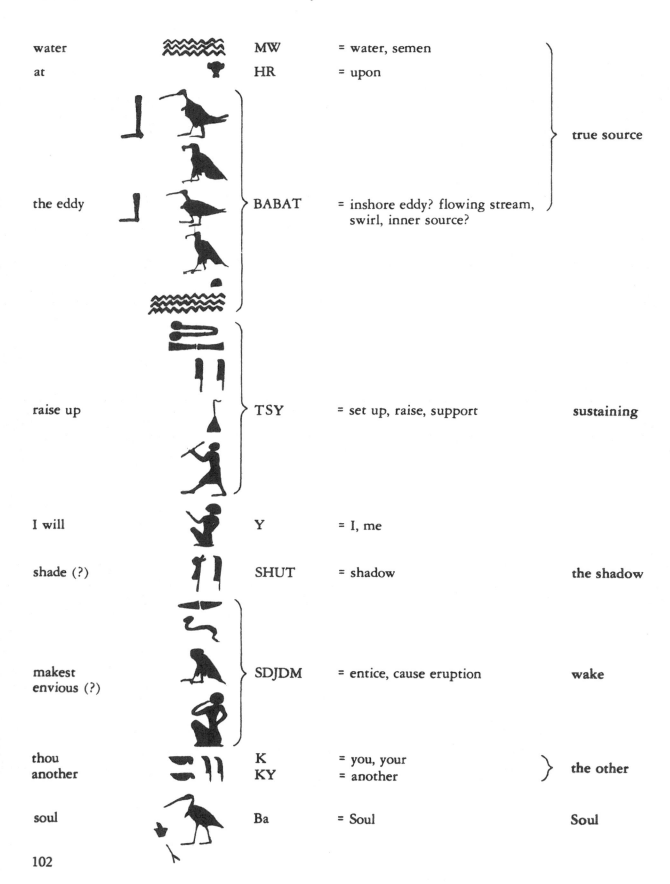

102

Faulkner	Dictionary		Reed

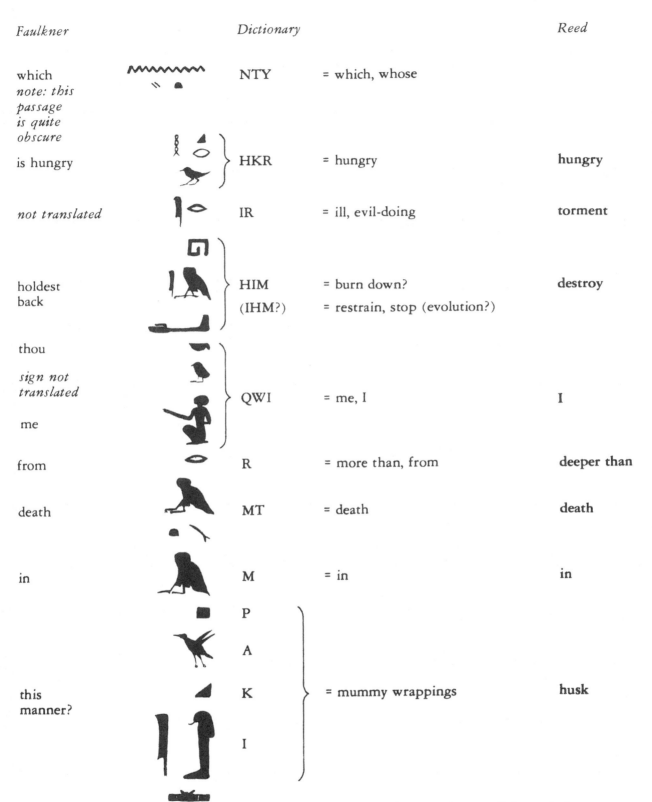

Faulkner		Dictionary		Reed
which *note: this passage is quite obscure*		NTY	= which, whose	
is hungry		HKR	= hungry	hungry
not translated		IR	= ill, evil-doing	torment
holdest back		HIM (IHM?)	= burn down? = restrain, stop (evolution?)	destroy
thou *sign not translated* me		QWI	= me, I	I
from		R	= more than, from	deeper than
death		MT	= death	death
in		M	= in	in
this manner?		P A K I	= mummy wrappings	husk

It is not my desire, by showing these parallel translations, to put a renowned Egyptologist to ridicule. Although Egyptology today is dry and lifeless like ashes, it has an important role: it keeps the fire of Egypt from extinction. Without the relentless and patient labor of the Egyptologists, the world would never have been able to come in contact with Ancient Egypt. Without the much disputed translations and dictionaries, the libraries and museums, new generations would not have the facilities they have today to contact the wisdom of Egypt. Unfortunately, many of them behave like builders who fall so in love with their building that they will not allow people to move in.

Clarifying the text of the classical *Lëbensmude*, which hitherto has been renowned for its obscurity, the translator does not pretend to demonstrate the superiority of some new translating skill, but a much more interesting fact: without the understanding of the underlying relationships of the symbolical themes which form the Ancient Egyptian myth, reading of all but the most straightforward hieroglyphs is virtually impossible. The thought expressed by the hieroglyphic words can only be understood through the basic structures inherent in the symbolism of the myth and does not yield itself to simple dictionary classifications. The misreading of a single word can obscure the sense of an entire text.

Failing to recognize IAI, the Great Ass, Faulkner in line 43 of the text, borrows an 'n' from the word above to form 'NIAI', and comments that 'NIAI' is of unknown meaning. Yet, IAI, the Great Ass is the Rebel of the Soul. This Great Ass found in several monuments and texts, is a recognized form of the sun god with ass's ears. Faulkner finds nineteen such 'corrections' in this text, setting off a chain reaction, like somebody who, eager to inherit a castle, murders a rich aunt, then, eliminating witness by witness, proceeds to murder her maid, then the butler, then the gardener, then the cook and finally, to erase all traces, must set fire to the castle itself.

Some scholars may say that I, on the contrary, have read too much sense into this text and that all the demonstrated consistency should be ascribed to the translator. I would be very proud of a compliment such as this, but must return it to where it belongs, as an 'offering to the temples'.

Introduction
to the Commentary

In the succeeding pages, we shall follow step by step, the emotional exposition and the philosophical conclusion of the most vital, eternal problem of man: his individual destiny. In a dialogue, a hypothetical man in 'despair' explores the possibilities of 'having his own way' in life.

Persuaded that the papyrus is an initiatic text, I have followed its line of argument in its intellectual and moral implications without concern for the precise reasons for the man's despair. I have not found any indication in the text of a personal reason for the despair of this man. On the contrary, the text clearly indicates the degenerate state of the society in which the man refuses to live and implies the lack of spiritual guidance after the traditional Great Sage and his 'disciple' have gone. It is possible that the man is mourning the death of his spiritual master and the theme of the papyrus would consequently suggest an analogy with the death of Socrates but we have nothing except an allusion (p.00) to support this idea. It appears, however, that overpowered by doubt and fear, lacking spiritual guidance and support the desperate man finally turns to his inner self and finds certitude in his own heart.

The structure of this dialogue and its conclusion are proof in themselves of its initiatic nature. For if this were not the case, the man's cry of despair would not be refuted so consummately in the replies of the Soul. The dialectical exchange of arguments and replies provoke the crisis in the man to rise, culminate, and fall into silent acceptance at the end. Previous interpretations have seen this text only as a pessimistic lament because the replies of the Soul have never been translated correctly. It is as though a Platonic dialogue were translated without the replies of Socrates. One can therefore understand that the content of the papyrus was judged as obscure and contradictory.

This dialogue, between the man and his soul, as we shall see from its symbolical implications is a masterly philosophical duel between inner knowledge and doubt.

It may seem strange that some short sentences in the papyrus often have long explanations in the commentary. However, those 'short sentences' relate to definite mythological themes and yield sense only through them. To appreciate the development of the argument and therefore the depth of its conclusion, one must understand how these mythological themes relate to the papyrus. It is through such long explanations that we arrive at a consistent interpretation, they therefore prove themselves necessary.

Duel between inner knowledge and doubt

AMIT

Commentary

1

The original papyrus of this text was discovered with its first section missing. The two opening lines of the existing texts are torn and incomplete. They have not been included in this translation. They read: '. . . you . . . saying . . . their tongues shall not be partial . . . the guilty . . . retribution. Their tongues shall not be partial . . .'

As one can judge from the text which follows, this broken sentence denotes an already advanced state of argument between the man and his soul. Unable to dissuade the man from his intention to end his life, the soul threatens 'Their tongues shall not be partial', referring to the forty-two judges of Osiris, before whom the man will have to answer for the offense of taking his own life.

The judgement of Osiris takes place on the 'Island of Fire' — the mystical heart of the world. Upon the balance, a man's heart is measured against the truth, symbolized by a feather. The trial decides between the alternatives: will the man be thrown to the monster AMIT to be reabsorbed into the bowels of the earth or will he be justified and released into the next stage of his spiritual evolution. It is not possible within the confines of this commentary to study the many aspects of that trial, but it is necessary to mention that the destiny of a man, which is determined by that trial, can be a new reincarnation after a long or shorter period, a final spiritual birth or final destruction. This latter possibility seems to be at the base of the soul's threat and consequently of the man's fear. It appears, judging by the soul's symbolical allusions, that suicide is an act which is punished by the 'loss of the soul' or irrevocable disintegration.

2

This phrase refers to the preceding text in which the soul, having tired of fruitless arguments, resorts to threat. The man realizes that he will have to bear the judgement alone, severed from his soul, and this prospect frightens him. This oldest known ancestor of Hamlet fears the consequences of suicide, but unlike Hamlet, his fear is not caused by his uncertainty and doubt in the reality of the afterlife; his fear is caused by the certitude that there will be a trial awaiting on the 'other side'.

3

In despair, the man wants only to end his life. Yet, he is anxious to obtain an agreement from his soul to insure his transcendence into the dimension of eternal life. It seems strange that, though ready to commit the most rebellious of all acts, the man cannot bear to envisage it without the blessing of his soul! Clearly, we are faced here with a strange form of suicide. A modern man, in despair, not believing in transcendence, asks no one's permission to die. Obviously, this ancient Egyptian did not conceive of suicide as we commonly understand it, but saw his death as an act of sacrifice. He wanted his soul to participate in this destructive act because he knew that only in union with his soul (BA) can his spiritual essence (KA) rise from his ashes like the 'Phoenix'. This 'Phoenix' will be his *Heir*. The concept of Heir, one of the main themes of Egyptian mythology, is central to the papyrus. The Heir is the final result of human genesis: a spiritual, indestructible form of life in which the soul is exalted. The image of this blissful state is haunting this desperate mind. The man understands that despair is blocking the way to his spiritual evolution. Unable to overcome this despair he tries to shortcut it.

A point worth mentioning here is that this papyrus demonstrates that the Egyptians understood reincarnation and its final goal of spiritual realisation in a more subtle way than is generally represented in the modern interpretation of the *Book of the Dead*. This man obviously did not believe that after dying, he would awake again in the same physical body. He was fully aware that he would never live in the same way again and herein lies the meaning of his sacrifice. He hoped to keep his spiritual essence actively alive in a 'quickened' process of transmutation by his willing death.

Phoenix — the exalted soul

4

The man refers to his body as a net. In this net he must enmesh his soul. We shall find later in the text an amazing fact. He also refers to *his* body as the *soul's* body, in which he, the mental being, is a destructive foreigner. Although referring to the same physical phenomenon, the body, Egypt again differs from us. For Egypt, the body is like the cosmos, a network of functions. Organs stand for celestial bodies, their interconnection sustains life. But although the function of the body was to sustain life, this was not considered the body's ultimate goal: rather, it was to act as a net in which its *Hidden Dweller* — the soul — is caught as a prey and ultimately exalted. This exaltation of the soul is a mystical, irrational process. The net and its prey are really one being.

In Egyptian papyri, we often find a *net* with birds caught in it. Upon the net, however, stands victoriously, the BENU bird, the phoenix. The soul encompasses the mystery of oneness. Its body is the net, in it is the prey and the victorious Hidden Dweller. Our man turns this irrational (mystical) image into a rational process, in which only *he* has the power to provide the opportunity for his soul to realise its own purpose by his 'sacrificial' death.

5

Inextricably, fear gives rise to aggression. The man now threatens his soul, saying that it will be judged for the man's crime by the Court of Osiris. For as the mother is responsible for her child's ill behavior, the soul will be responsible for the misbehavior of the man.

6

A lacuna has swallowed the beginning of the sentence. After indicating the 'dead end' awaiting the Soul if it does not 'stay' with him in his sacrificial death, the man now behaves as a politician would in an election campaign. He presents the blissful image of an alternative possibility. The Soul will penetrate him at the moment of death, animating his spiritual essence, the KA — rising on the other side as the Heir, the exalted spiritual being. It will perform the miracle of the Creator.

The catch

BENU (phoenix)

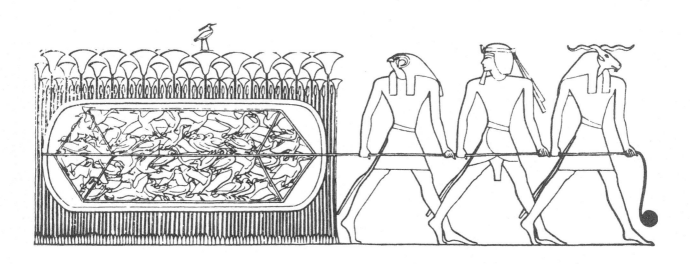

The Soul encompasses the mystery of oneness. Its body is the net; in it is the prey and the victorious Hidden Dweller, the phoenix

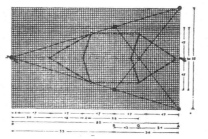

The net is a demonstration of the theory of Pythagoras

The man compares his soul, in its creative capacity, to the NHPU, the Potter, translated in the poem, 'creator.' NHPU is one of the names of Thoth (creative thought). In its function as 'potter' the mind fashions its own being. But the Divine Potter of Egypt is also identified with the BA (soul) of RA (sun). The 'potter' therefore stands for the mind and for the soul. When our man, referring to this potter, says, 'he extracts Himself from himself', he points at the Soul extracting and animating its own KA essence through the agency of his sacrifice. He uses, throughout this text, the mythological imagery symbolizing assimilation, the main function of life.

The 'Assimilation into the Divine' is one of the main themes of the *Book of the Dead.* Assimilation, in its absract aspect, is creative magic. By the same 'magic' in the walls of the small intestine, the offered (sacrificed) food becomes flesh, blood and ultimately thought. The man pretends that by ending his life, he is enacting the very same process of assimilation; offering his flesh to be transformed into the Heir. To show the error of his thoughts and therefore to appreciate the subtle nature of this text, it is necessary to examine the relationship between the BA (soul) and its magnetic essence, the KA. Hidden in the body, the KA lives as a root, its tree is the soul, its fruit is the mental being. The fruit must give its life to the seed. The mental being must sacrifice its own existence, the personality — for its 'seed' — the mystical Heir.

It appears from all mythological documentation, that the mental being has the important role of acting as a bridge between the two dimensions. On one side stands the potential root (KA), on the other, the realized seed (Heir). Without the fruit (mental being), the root (KA) cannot form its seed: therein lies the sacred role of the mental being, so well understood by Ancient Egypt. Like the fruit of a tree, it must 'offer' its life to its own seed. Consequently, the mental being must at a certain stage of its evolution, offer its life to its own seed. But the subtle aspect of this offering was grossly simplified by the man. His error could be described as an intellectual rationalization of initiatic symbolism. 'Self-creation' in Egypt, as in all Inner Traditions, is the goal of initiation. The mystical, human offering is central to this goal.

Initiation treats the realization of this goal on two levels: the natural way and the 'quickened path'. Its symbolism reflects both levels and can be interpreted accordingly. From the viewpoint of the natural way, a symbolic image is literally read in its physical implication. From the 'quickened' viewpoint it is read as an element of an evocative mystical language.

Our desperate man commits the error of mixing levels and consequently, their symbolism. This papyrus treats the problems arising from this error which have remained with us, even to this day.

In the natural way, the seed is put back into the ground to sprout again, indicating a cycle of rebirth as a road to gradual illumination. In the quickened path, this cycle is by-passed and the goal is attained by process of extraction of oneself from oneself.

The desperate man has confused the two ways. Refusing his natural mat-

NUT, the soul — or tree of life

uration he refers to the symbolism of the quickened path as a justification for his 'philosophical' suicide. But he gives to this mystical symbolism a literal interpretation. We can illustrate the error by analyzing one of the symbolical images of the quickened path of Egypt: the hieroglyph of an arm (representing the act) which holds a closed lotus flower. The closed lotus was exoterically linked to death. In graphic representations, a person smelling the closed lotus flower was commonly understood as being deceased. The students of the Sacred Text saw, however, the same image differently, they saw in it the act of extracting (symbolised by smelling) the essence (life) of the closed lotus.

This symbolic image brings a new element to our mind, the lotus bloom. The fruit offers its life to the seed, but the bloom precedes the fruit. The lotus is the symbolic image for both maturity and exaltation. If we compare our mental being to the fruit, we must conclude that the condition preceding the conversion of the fruit into seed must be maturity, or exaltation. Further, we have to conclude that only the mature fruit offers its life to the seed — and likewise, only the exalted mental being offers its life to its Heir.

The bloom of the mental being is its individuality. It reaches maturity by a full expansion of its individual potential. The hieroglyph of the arm holding the closed lotus indicates the act of turning the energy of blooming inwards thus bringing about the quickening of the seed. A mystical, new direction is given to the blooming which exalts the mature individual potential. Apparently, the blooming is by-passed, but in reality it is turned inwards. This exaltation is symbolised by the image of the head coming out of the lotus bloom. It expresses the outcome of the mystical direction given to the bloom, and new birth into light. This birth does not come from a new root after the seed is put back into the ground, but sprouts directly from the inner bloom.

In both the natural and the quickened way, all the stages of evolution must be passed through before illumination. The quickened way is not a simple short-cut but a conscious redirection or inversion of the energies of evolution. In both ways life is necessary and cannot be by-passed. In the living heart its seed sprouts, taking the heart's life, the awareness. It becomes by that union a living light.

Man holding a closed lotus flower: he chooses the quickened path

7

After having tempted his soul by the attractive prospect of the blissful beyond the man now uses logical argument. If life is transitory, a cycle of births and deaths, why bother living? If everything decays, even huge trees, why not destroy our weakness, rebellion and misery? Suicide is a shortcut to eternity.

Putting forward this line of reasoning, the man expresses a degenerate attitude similar to the one which, in India, has led to the neglect of physical life in the hope of some imaginary spirituality. It is interesting to observe that this dialogue between doubt and inner knowledge seems to explore consecutive phases of self-deceit (rebellion and despair) which precede real understanding of spiritual evolution. It looks as if the ancient Egyptians understood the phases of that evolution as well as we understand the phases of chicken pox or measles.

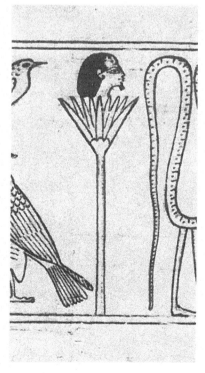

New life sprouting from the inner bloom

In this light, this papyrus could be compared to a psycho-medical handbook. It is important to point out that these phases and crises also corresponded to the twelve hours and gates of the voyage of the boat of the Sun through the underworld.

8

Carried away with his own bravery, the man now pleads his case with his soul like the devil's advocate before the court of Osiris. He challenges the very principle of measure — Djehuti — to judge him (if he dares)! Djehuti is an aspect of Toth, the 'god of peace between the gods.' (i.e. proportion, balance, judgement). The man is challenging the divine judge of the court of Osiris and putting his trust in Khonsu to defend him, in Ra to 'hear' his case and in Isdes to absolve him. By his elaborate plea, however, he really has nothing new to say. His aims could be reduced to one phrase: Please let me die! But self-deceit is the shadow of truth and can therefore have as many aspects as the truth itself. The man explores all its combinations like a thief trying to open a safe. His pleas are based on his obsession with the 'quickened path'. He cries out: 'let Djehuti judge me by the balance of natural laws! By that criterion, I am guilty indeed, for in the natural path, balance perpetuates sanity'. But, he then continues cunningly: 'in the quickened path equilibrium must be cast away, sanity rejected and life itself sacrificed to the search for mystical oneness. Therefore the mystical redeemer, Khonsu, will defend me, for he is the scribe of Maat, the Truth Above all Laws.' Maat is symbolized by both the feather and the sickle. By its sickle, Maat harvests life for its grain of light. This grain is the essence of life itself, more powerful therefore, than life. As the highest function, above natural laws which perpetuate order, Maat's scribe, Khonsu (Cons-ciousness) will take his side in the court. For doesn't he, like Khonsu, tread the solitary path beyond nature and its laws, guided only by the sickle of the truth?

The man then calls to Ra to hear his words for it is Ra himself who guides the Holy Barque through the underworld ('the dark night of the soul'). Beyond nature and the fear of dying, he steers it towards the new dawn. The man believes therefore that he is mystically guided by Ra and that the act of plunging into death would make it possible for him to climb on the Barque of Ra and thus be assimilated into the Sun.

Djehuti

Khonsu

RA

Isdes

Even though he plans to take his own life, he believes that there is no doubt that he will be absolved. He turns to Isdes, the Intelligence of the Heart. Isdes, the spiritualised intellect symbolised by a baboon, sits atop the scales of judgement. Upon the scales, the man's heart is weighed against the light, symbolized by a feather. By its own weight, the heavy heart will pull a man to be reabsorbed into the bowels of the earth. By its 'light', it will ascend into the spiritual dimension. But in his case, he is certain Isdes will intercede. Isdes, the intelligence of the heart, is the baboon sacred to Toth. The man calls on this baboon to lift the weight from his heart and thus redress the balance in his favor. He claims that Isdes, the intellect, is responsible for his vision of the greatest of all mysteries; the will to die for the light. On the balance, opposite his heavy heart rests the feather, symbolising the light. How can this same light condemn him for offering his own life to reach it?

The will to die for the light takes in the man's imagination the form of the Lord of Transformations. In the Egyptian myth, the Lord of Transformations was one of the titles of the mummified falcon god Sokar, a god symbolically evoking death for resurrection.

The falcon drops upon his prey to then ascend, carrying animal blood to the sun. The man thinks that in death his heavy heart will similarly ascend offering its blood to the sun.

113

9

The answer of the soul is comparable in its tone to a mother's scolding. It accuses the man of fretting over life like a man attached to his wealth (Lord of Heaps), and warns: NEFA is 'one foot off the ground.' To understand the warning, we must define the word NEFA. NEFA is usually translated "the one yonder" or "the deceased". Egyptology defines a number of Egyptian words with the term 'deceased'. But if all these words had had the same meaning to the Egyptians, they would not be differentiated as they are. NEFA is a demonstrative pronoun indicating a carrier. It does not indicate the sublime essence itself, but the temporary carrier of it. Using the symbolism of the egg, one could say that NEFA corresponds to the inner membrane of the egg. Death breaks the shell (personality), but the nucleus is left protected by the membrane, which carries it until the formation of a new shell.

NEFA is the subtle, psychic membrane of our being, and its dissolution is much slower than that of the physical body. It carries the Name, which could be compared to a formula for reincarnation. In death, it is the brainless, mindless shadow. Suicide would expose it to the loss of its protective, magnetic Name. It would then become exposed, susceptible of attraction into any orbit and liable to be used for "evil" purposes.

10

The 'Name' in Ancient Egypt was considered to be a blueprint of being and as such, the key to evolution be it reincarnation or final liberation. As a chemical formula holds the key to a substance, the Name holds the key to a man. If the NEFA, its carrier, is cut away from the man through suicide, the effect is comparable to a pregnant womb being cut away from its lifegiving mother, the soul. The soul warns that by his suicide, NEFA would be released and his spiritual potential would be destroyed.

11

The man carries the intellect; the NEFA carries the man's continuation. The soul warns, only if a man is allowed to continue evolving, can the intellect reach the heart.

The Egyptian word 'AFD' is not yet clearly defined by the dictionaries of Egyptology. Its attributed root meanings are: 'attractive' and 'leading'. Both evoke in the context of this papyrus a 'magnetic leader' which I have translated as intellect. Intellect, as a concept, was not specified in Egypt as a separate notion but was an aspect of the magnetic essence of the KA. The union of the intellect and the heart is the effect of spiritual evolution; the upstream struggle, leading to the Haven. Only after having resolved inner contradiction while alive, can the illuminated man reach in death, the Haven Beyond.

12

As he could not impress his soul by threat or temptation, the man playing 'honest' appeals to pity. He uses the image of the accomplished sage, the one 'within his pyramid,' succeeded by his spiritual heir on the day of his death — only to draw attention to the misery of his own failure to heed his soul.

13

Like an actor who identifies himself with a negative hero, taking morbid

Intellect (the KA as 'SHU')
separating earth (GEB)
from sky (NUT)

The way to the Haven

pleasure in it, the man now identifies himself with the Great Ass IAI. In the Egyptian myth, IAI is a sun god with ass's ears and represents a negative aspect of the sun. The sun is the source of life and movement. The ass is a living symbol of opposition to movement. The sun with ass's ears represents the source of obstinacy and rebellion. The man cries out: 'In this body, which is yours, I am the progeny of IAI.' In this organism, the body, which is a network of harmonic interconnections, the man identifies himself with the source of obstinacy and rebellion. The psychological awareness, risen as an obstinate, rebellious second self in the body and translated in the text as 'the Other' — is called in the Egyptian text K-Ki. Saying, 'I call forth "the Other,"' this man, although conscious of his own rebellion, does not identify himself with this rebel K-Ki, but with the causal flame of rebellion. It is typical of the intellectual to believe in his own objectivity; this part of the papyrus points at that delusion. The desperate man does not identify himself with K-Ki, the Other, waking as an half opened eye in the depths of the network of his own being, which he faces without understanding. He does not say: I am the Other in your body, a shadow caught in the labyrinth of my own illusion. If the man said that, then he could not claim an objective value for his proposal to the soul. For admitting that he was a phenomenon, such as that shadow, risen as an effect of the 'negative sun', he would have to add: Therefore you must dismiss my argument as it results from my vision relative to something beyond my control. This confession would end the argument. But the man does not want or cannot face such truth. He shouts, 'I am the flame, the progeny of the negative sun,' inferring, 'I am the sun itself.' He places himself in the causal dimension, whilst pushing forward a claim of egotistic origin. He is definitely mixing the 'levels' and therefore he says: 'In you I call forth the Other, O Soul, unawakened.' The man here evokes the mythical ocean, like the soul, source of all life, yet unaware. In its depths, awakes the psychological awareness, a flame separating itself from its origin. This flame, IAI, is an aspect of sun. Can the sun 'cool'?! He causes the Other to burst forth, a pyromaniac, who sets the soul alight, by discord and unrest, consuming 'the true source in sustaining the shadow.'

The man believes that, like in an electical short circuit, the vital flame has been tragically deviated. The effect of this destruction will be deeper than death. It will destroy the soul in its 'husk.'

Inner conflict in the form of the Black Ass

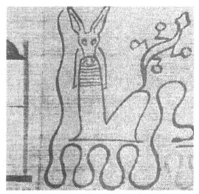

The Holy Ass upon his throne, the redeemed serpent of rebellion

IAI, the source of obstinacy and rebellion

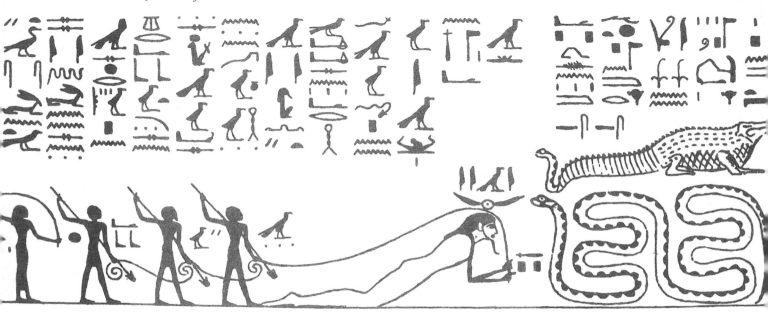

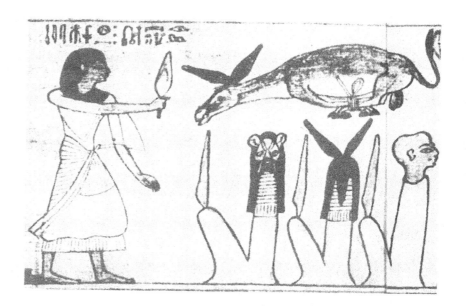

The destructive fire of the Great Ass, or inner conflict, fettered and thus raised by the act of redemption

To the Ancient Egyptians, natural death did not effect the soul, for natural death destroys neither the name nor the KA. Only by destroying the name, can the soul, the mystical unity of this name and its KA, be disintegrated. The man who would in fact by suicide destroy his Name and therefore lose his soul, pretends, on the contrary, that by living he would destroy his soul. Therefore, he identifies himself with the destructive fire of IAI, the Great Ass. By self-sacrifice, he believes he would put an end to this 'Ass,' which has taken possession of his mind and which threatens to destroy in the husk (his body), the soul. I have translated the Egyptian word 'mummy cloth' by the word 'husk,' because the concept of mummy is today very far from its original meaning. For Egypt, a mummy is a seed, wrapped for eternity. Its wrappings are like a husk is to a seed, a protective skin. Predicting to his soul a bitter end caused by his own destructive mentality, the man is forgetting that inner conflict (the flame of IAI) behind its destructive appearance, has a deeper meaning and should be observed as the 'creative drama' of spiritual evolution.

In life as in antique mystery plays, tragic events indicate some deeper, hidden truth. The man, behaving as an actor, mistakes the play for life to the point of actually attempting to murder the hero. But as the seed splits to sprout, so man, split by his own inner conflict, can ultimately evolve by assessing the mystical nature of that conflict, which is the hidden root of all despair.

In recognizing the propelling potential of inner contradiction, man can build a powerful motor. Nowadays, this possibility has been explored by technology, but in its gross (intellectual) aspect only, and separate from the 'heart.' Although producing great benefits from the exploitation of sources of energy, based on 'polarity', it is leading us to annihilation.

But man has the possibility of understanding his own 'polarity' or inner conflict, which could then become a vehicle to wisdom called by the Egyptians, 'the Intelligence of the Heart.' Through an understanding of

Ancient Egyptian thought the Western intellectual could explore his energies of conflict. Instead we suppress them, only to have them later erupt in irrational aggression and despair. First, like our desperate man, he must recognize that the cause of his despair lies in the intellectual presumption of 'objectivity'. Our Ancient Egyptian, in his crisis, shows much similarity to the modern rebel. At the root of the intellectual rejection of the 'Irrational' is a fear of the loss of identity. The intellect cannot face its own fallacy; rather it will turn to suicide or destruction in order to preserve the dream image of its own causal nature. The will to die in our desperate man is of a similar nature. He perceives that the 'Other', a shadow in his soul, is an obstacle between him and illumination. He doesn't have the heart to discover who that 'Other' is and therefore fails to recognize in himself the first stirrings of the awareness which, by reaching the heart, would bring illumination. This obstacle or shadow has been called by different names in different traditions, but they all refer to psychological awareness, a rebel in the soul. All traditions are concerned with the delicate process of reintegrating this 'prodigal son' into the Harmony (soul); but rarely does one find such clear, intelligent assessment of this inner conflict as in Egypt, where it is viewed as the very expression of 'sprouting'. Many spiritual teachers indicate the inner conflict as a negative state and recommend spiritual tranquillizers. Rare are those who push the initiate to assess the nature of his inner disorder prior to working on its solution. To assess one's own inner conflict in its mystical essence is the theme of this papyrus. Suicide is only one image of self-deceit. There are many forms of suicide and its physical aspect, being obvious, is the least dangerous. In fact, both concepts of 'sacrifice' and 'suicide' are of intellectual origin. Intellect, in its culminating phase, fires the inner conflict between the individual and his soul. This conflict can lead to suicide or deceptive 'sacrifice'. Paradoxically, individuality in its extreme aspect represents a form of suicide. In Ancient Egypt, the initiate, on the threshold of the Inner Temple, had to visualize this very threshold as an abyss. From the abyss of his own inner conflict, he had to emerge like the mythical god TUM, creating himself from himself.

Mystical fear of the loss of identity

14

After a long confession which predicts the soul's end because of his irredeemable negativity, the man once again implores his soul to hear his plea: to allow his premature death and in this way 'assist' in creating his spiritual Heir. 'He' will rise from his tomb and present the offering, his life, on the day of burial. This human offering, he thinks, will open the way to Eternal Life.

15

The reply of the soul combines tenderness with inevitable sarcasm: for not only is his dream image naive, but it will lead him in the direction opposite to his goal. Instead, he will be 'offered' to the vultures, thrown on the hill and reabsorbed into the earth. He will never ascend that hill, a mythical image for both abstraction and evolution. Unable to reach its summit, he will not reach the understanding of the twofold nature of creation indicated by the relationship between rising and setting sun. Illumination, like the sun has its day and its night. In the human dimension, despair is night and like the night, has its function. The soul is suggesting gently a thought which will be developed throughout the rest of the text. It is directing the man's attention to the light beyond duality, from which both day and night emanate. The night is thus incorporated into the Light, although *rationally* incompatible with the day. The sunset has its spiritual function, as does decline and despair in man.

In this speech, the soul appeals to the man's reason, by putting forward the value of life which the man has underrated in the hope of finding glory in the never-ending day of Beyond. In sustaining its own mental being, the man, the soul diplomatically points out that even the great sages of antiquity, the pyramid-builders, cannot protect men from decline; when the sun starts sinking into the night, even their 'sceptres' fall to dust. But mystically, Light is perpetuated as the virtues of creation are perpetuated, in the pyramids. In this passage, the original text is symbolically complex. The relationship between the hieroglyphic words creates a thought impossible to translate directly. The word NFR, for example, is used twice: once in the plural and once in the singular. This word translated as 'virtue' implies both potency and quality. The interplay between the plural 'virtues' and singular 'virtue' creates a simple and accessible image in the ancient Egyptian language. It points to the pyramid as an edifice by which the virtues of nature are unified. This unification is indicated by the use of the singular 'virtue'.

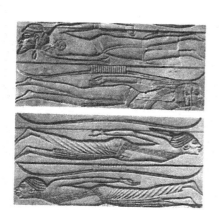

The unawakened

The great builders, shaping stone like clay, edified the virtues of creation in the pyramid and in themselves and therefore were 'like gods.' Those great sages have transcended the causal dimension; yet on earth, the same 'virtues' (laws) of nature still continue causing the rise and fall of all things as the sun rises and sets. Inextricably, in a transitional period, when the sun goes 'down', disorder reigns. Moral values fall. Degeneracy rules like a dark flood, swallows the *unawakened* left upon the shore of that mythical river which we find in many of the ancient traditions: a flow that nothing can stop and nothing, except knowledge, can cross. The soul evokes this mythical reality by the image of the *unawakened* dead upon the river bank. The flood of man's despair has drowned him. The heat of his own rebellion has destroyed him. Fish feed on him in shallow water.

16

After telling him that men of greater value than he had suffered from the world, the soul now says that he must gain insight into the dangers of his attitude, advising him to search for understanding in order to overcome despair. To illustrate the danger of his ignorance and presumption, the soul tells him two allegorical tales. Both of the tales begin by saying: 'There was a NDJSU,' a term indicating a commoner and also, in this case, a layman in the sacred science.

In the first story, a NDJSU follows all the precepts but does not achieve the goal. This story relates to the mythical field of transformations, where both the field and the plough are in man. The field is the ground where the KA is buried to be cultivated by the plougher. The goal of this cultivation is not the harvest, but the *offering* of the harvest to the soul. This offering is expressed in the ancient Egyptian myth as the Triumphal Day, the mythical festival of joy. By ploughing his field and loading his harvest into the barge, the man believed that the time of his Triumphal Day was close at hand. But a NDJSU, the commoner, is never found in the sacred texts offering his harvest upon the altar of eternity. For any

In the spiritual evolution of man, ploughing symbolises the creative use of negative tension; reaping symbolises the outcome, new life (the crocodile of tension and the woman, the life-giver, bow to each other)

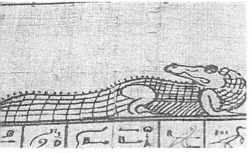

The chequered pattern on the crocodile represents the net of creative tension

ancient Egyptian, the use of the word NDJSU in this context would clearly indicate the final outcome of the tale. The harvest in the hands of the NDJSU is a dangerous possession, for the way to the festival leads him into the storm. This storm, gathering from the north (head) symbolizes consciousness threatened by the intellectual rebellion. In this moment, the NDJSU, not yet ready to rule his intellect by the wisdom of the heart, is in danger of destruction. Although aware of this approaching 'storm' coming from the north, the man in the tale loses control. His heart sinks like the sun, bringing darkness. In his darkness, he loses his harvest. His knowledge is uprooted and without light, he cannot find his way any more. It is not by chance that this tragedy occurs on the Lake of the Crocodile, which is also the mythical Lake of Fire. Symbolically, 'crocodile' stands for creative contraction. This reptile is a huge muscular tail armed with a jaw (muscles operate only through contraction; while tension is present, they contract, executing movement). The 'crocodile' gods in ancient Egyptian myth symbolize different aspects of the creative tension. This tension gives life and also takes it. It provokes conflict in man, and when measured, brings harmony. Our heart through its measured contraction, sustains our life, and losing measure, takes it. The judgement of the right measure or 'balance' is symbolized in the myth by the scales of the Court of Osiris. This court is placed upon an island on that very Lake of Fire where the poor NDJSU loses his harvest and his spiritual inheritance. Over that stormy Lake of the Crocodile, rational knowledge cannot find its way. It cannot master the 'crocodile' and gets eaten by it. The only leader in this dangerous journey is the 'Intelligence of the Heart' a secret drummer who gives the right 'beat' to our evolution. Like the Pace Maker in our physical heart, this intelligence is independent from the brain. The beat of our heart is set by electrical impulses generated by a complex of nerve-like cells called the Pace Maker. Surprisingly, this Pace Maker is the only nerve in our body which does not depend on the brain, for if a heart is cut out of a man, it still beats.

A man can study scriptures and follow methods guided by masters, but when the sun sinks, unless he finds Inner Knowledge, he will be lost: his 'wife' and 'children' will fall to the crocodiles.

In this tale, the sequence of events seems logical at first sight, but in examining the detail we encounter the Absurd. This is a typical feature of Ancient Egyptian sacred texts. By using contradiction, an element of the Absurd, they draw attention to a deeper meaning and prevent literal interpretation.

The text says that his wife and children were eaten by the double crocodile Henti, then states that those children have *seen* the face of the Henti before they lived and they were smashed in the egg. This absurd image of children seeing Henti before living and smashed in the egg, indicates a

Sebek, the Lord of Death

Mercurius Senex in his vessel of transformations

It is the jaw of the crocodile which holds the vessel *of transformations*

deeper meaning. Not only his physical reincarnations (wife) are lost as 'she will never ever return from the Beyond,' but also his spiritual inheritance (children) will be forever lost, before realizing their potential (smashed in the egg). The text clearly indicates 'children' in plural, separate from the 'wife' and excludes the possibility of a pregnant woman being devoured by the crocodile.

The Henti crocodile is a form of Saturn. It is depicted by the image of two crocodiles. This double contraction relates to the inner conflict in its final stage; it symbolizes the final destruction at the end of 'time' or a cycle, the outcome of which is either transcendence or complete annihilation. This form of Saturn in alchemy is Mercurius Senex.

The soul warns the man, by this tale, that his self-induced premature death would throw him into the jaws of Henti, from which he will never emerge.

17

The first tale is concluded by the second tale in which the soul laconically exposes the man to an image of his self-righteous presumption. He is compared to a NDJSU, hungry for the reward (evening meal) for his daily labors. This impatient NDJSU, stalking out in rage, is indeed comparable to the man of our papyrus, angry with the world and life itself and wanting only his reward.

Many adepts of wisdom are also comparable to this NDJSU. Their bitterness results from their spiritual immaturity. By this conclusive image, the soul reduces the escapist speeches of the man to zero. As in a chess game, each of his moves is checked by the same obstacle: truth.

18

The exposé of the soul breaks the man. He bursts out crying in anguish like a child. But even in this deepest anguish, the man does not yet accept defeat. Under his tears, he uses the soul's warning only to exalt his misery. This man is passing through a womb of darkness, the hour before the dawn. In alchemy, that hour is called 'nigredo'. In the Egyptian Book of the Dead, this dark hour is described in chapter CLXXV. It could be compared to a crucial stage in baking. The baker and the bread are one. If the fire is too strong, the bread will burn. Fueling his lament with the soul's warnings, the man is raising the temperature dangerously.

19

After crying aimlessly, the man starts blaming the world for the dead end to which his life has come. He describes the hopeless state of society (in some ways reminiscent of today.) His despair builds up as he evokes the disappearance of the traditional great sage, 'the Serene Heart'. The man adds that 'he who follows him is no more.' It seems that the death of the spiritual master may have been the original symbolical pivot around which the initiation of this papyrus was built. This death would account for both the loss of guidance and the desperate need for the man to find the inner source of wisdom. The man cries out that he is left alone without guidance and therefore calls death to relieve him from a life which has become a torment.

20

In the thick darkness of his lost faith, the man is slowly intoning his swansong. 'He Who Dwells Within' will absolve his crime. The man has reached the climax of delusion. He now composes a hymn to his Heir. He cries out for this Heir to rise in the Holy Barque of Night. In this boat which sails on the darkest night of the new moon, he will give back to the Temples which initiated him in the mysteries, the greatest of all offerings: his own life.

The man's speech is now exhausted. He really has nothing to add and keeps reminding RA that his death means Eternal Life.

21

Like a violent stream, which, after rushing down a steep rock dissolves itself in the sea, the man's voice disappears. The replies of the soul throughout the text, by their majestic certitude and symbolical associations, build an understanding which is meant to condition the right vital attitude.

The answer of the soul seems at the first glance surprisingly colloquial by contrast to the poetic language of the man. As if joking, it dismisses his misery, reminding him that the power which supports him belongs to the soul. Many are the dangers of self-deceiving practices which promise a quick step into the Beyond. The soul says, 'Forget the Beyond.' In the 'celebration' of the Beyond, the harvest of life is consumed. The mature fruit of life is 'offered.' But this offering is an act of mystical love and not of despair.

'As long as you burn, you belong to life.' These words of the soul indicate that the inner conflict provoking despair in man is far from its resolution. But it also indicates that life itself has the role of a cauldron in which man is prepared for his ultimate consummation. He has not yet passed the dark hour of transformation, and reached the maturity of a vision beyond life and death. In a living sage, death and life meet. But such sages are rare. Their becoming is far beyond human understanding. Their bodies are left to the earth like empty snakeskins.

One of the questions which arises directly from this Papyrus is how to understand Ancient Egyptian methods of spiritual evolution. One could think that the apparently simple answers of the soul dismiss the value of quickening one's progress. But that simplicity in language could be compared to the nakedness of a hermit confronted with a richly robed and drunken priest, frustrated in his spiritual ambition. The replies of the soul do not negate the quickened path, the true method is only being separated from the false. If the choice between the true and the false could be made by the logical, discerning quality alone, there would be on this earth more sages than fishes.

A tap, however efficient, gives no water unless connected to the main: if the system is leaky and rotten, the tap may produce poison while appearing to give sustenance. So the discerning intellect nourishes only if connected with the soul.

Our intellect is eager to define, to edify and therefore to limit. In its growth at a certain peak, the intellect, becoming stagnant, turns to a limiting aggression. In separating from his soul, the rebel turns against life. In Egypt, this *turning* was considered the right time for redemption.

The Ancient Egyptian myth, which describes the birth of the Redeemer, Anubis, gives us an insight into this dramatic *turning* or birth into higher consciousness. In this myth, the Jackal Dog is pursuing Set, the enemy of Light, who takes the form of a panther and escapes the dog. But the mother she-dog, Isis, sees the panther and catches up. Terrified of the wild bitch, the panther transforms himself into the dog, *his own pursuer*. But Isis digs her teeth into his back. Caught, Set cries, 'Why are you pursuing this poor dog *who does not exist?*' The myth then says: And this is

*Anubis, the Lord of Spiritual
Becoming, faces the monster of destruction (inexistence) under the balance of
truth*

how HE BECAME. 'He-Became' (IN PU) is the Egyptian name for Anubis, the first priest of Osiris. The Redeemer, (IN PU) comes to life by *seeing* his own 'inexistence.'

Our man in the papyrus, in his escapism, pretends that he is the Redeemer himself. Like Set, he transforms himself into his own 'pursuer' and hides his real nature behind the sublime. But his soul digs her teeth into his back and by those teeth of truth, he is forced like Set to admit his own fallacy (inexistence). In realising that he is not the causal principle, or sun, but only its effect, he will be born into a new dimension. Only by those 'teeth' of truth will he be assimilated into divine flesh.

*The first priest of Osiris in panther
skin*

*IN PU leading the 'dead' to
resurrection*

126

The circuitous path

The Heir

One could conclude that the modern intellectual will be born into wisdom when he recognizes his own phenomenal nature and, forgetting about his 'objectivity,' starts searching his own source.

To find the source, man must turn his boat around and navigate upstream. In this dramatic conflict he builds, step by step, the base for the Abode of the Beyond. The circuitous path of evolution and its goal, the Abode, remind us of the labyrinth concept, developed through the ages which followed Egypt. In many ancient and early Medieval monuments, this concept of 'circuitous path', sometimes called 'macaroni drawings' by art historians, is present, as a mute witness, to an universal truth. We find labyrinth lines carved on the floors of many Gothic cathedrals. Those carvings, barely perceptible in most cases, are a hidden warning present to all men entering the Edifice. They symbolize both the snare in which the mind is lost and the process of its evolvement. The labyrinth complex is linked both to the alchemical *temenos* and the alchemical bath. It is the enclosure (limitation, frame, body) in which a fire (polarized energy — conflict) is breaking up a unity (soul) to create a new unity (Heir).

Man is a field of transformations. In him, as in a wilderness, he has to clear the way and prepare the foundation for the Abode. The earth must be flat. Our flesh must be at rest.

Laying the foundation for the Abode

PEH, the below

The Abode is a living structure. The soul says, "Then united we shall form the Abode" and adds, "when *its* (the Abode's) HATY (forepart — above) is placed upon its PEH (hindpart — below)". HATY and PEH are the two parts of the mythical Lion. The HATY, its forepart, is the hieroglyph standing for the spiritual heart, i.e. orientation: upper regions of our being including the head. The PEH is the hieroglyph for the hindparts which stand for power, passion, rebellion, motion and achievement. Like a running lion, evolution is powered by the PEH and directed by HATY, its forepart. The living Abode, in which the two parts are reunited evokes the sphinx.

It was difficult to transmit all of those concepts in a literal translation of the sentence 'When its HATY is placed upon its PEH.' I have chosen therefore 'The Above is exalted by the Below' having in mind the well known: 'As Above so Below' from the Greek *'Hermetica.'*

The text then concludes, 'As found in the Scriptures.' It is interesting to compare the thought expressed in this original ancient Egyptian text with the *Hermetica,* a Medieval version of the possibly corrupted Greek transcript of a body of writings attributed to Hermes Trismegistus (Egyptian Toth). Both refer to a Canon of Egyptian sacred writings still in existence in the time of Clement of Alexandria and lost in the great fire of the Alexandrian Library.

The Greek, 'As Above, so Below' is a rational, equational comparison which includes separation. The Egyptian concept exposed in this papyrus refers to a mystical oneness. 'Its Above is placed upon its Below' (the forepart of a lion is placed upon the hindpart of a lion). Both the Below and the Above are here understood beyond their spatial dimension. The Below, in its relationship to the Above, is like coal in its relationship to the diamond. Similarly, the 'celestial king' stands upon the 'dragon' in the early Gothic cathedral. Today, the Below and its Above are no longer seen as one 'lion.'

We conceive each part as a totality and debate the existence of the other. The concept of PEH which has been conventionalized as 'evil' and its mutiple derivations, such as pessimism, rational philosophy, despair or anarchy evoke an absurd image of the world, ruled by a beheaded hindpart. Somehow, on the way from Egypt to our world, the 'lion' has been lost. But, from the midst of the desert of Egypt, the ageless Sphinx still calls for its resurrection. The voice of the soul proclaims to man that the 'lion' is found only when the HATY is upon the PEH.

The revelation of this ancient text is unique in mystical literature. It places rebellion within the Canon, as the crucial stage in spiritual transformation.

The dialogue between this rebel, the first in the history of literature, and his soul, demonstrates that the force of individualism, causing rebellion,

HATY, the above

is also the very source of spiritual redemption in man.

In 'rebellion' or separation from his soul, man creates individuality as a new psychological entity endowed with intellect, unknown in nature. This new entity is thrown like a drawbridge over the abyss, so that consciousness can step into the Beyond.

Recognizing that 'rebellion' is essential to the process of evolution, can the rebel endure? No, he is broken. He is no longer a rebel as he does no more than conform to the immutable law of transformation. *Seeing* this, the Rebel dies. The king is born. 'For its Above is exalted by its Below' as written in the scriptures.

The Rebel, symbolised by the head of the Ass, supports the Heir, born from reconciled contradiction (the two lions of yesterday and today) into Eternity

The Author's
Hieroglyphic Transcript
of the
Berlin Papyrus 3024

132

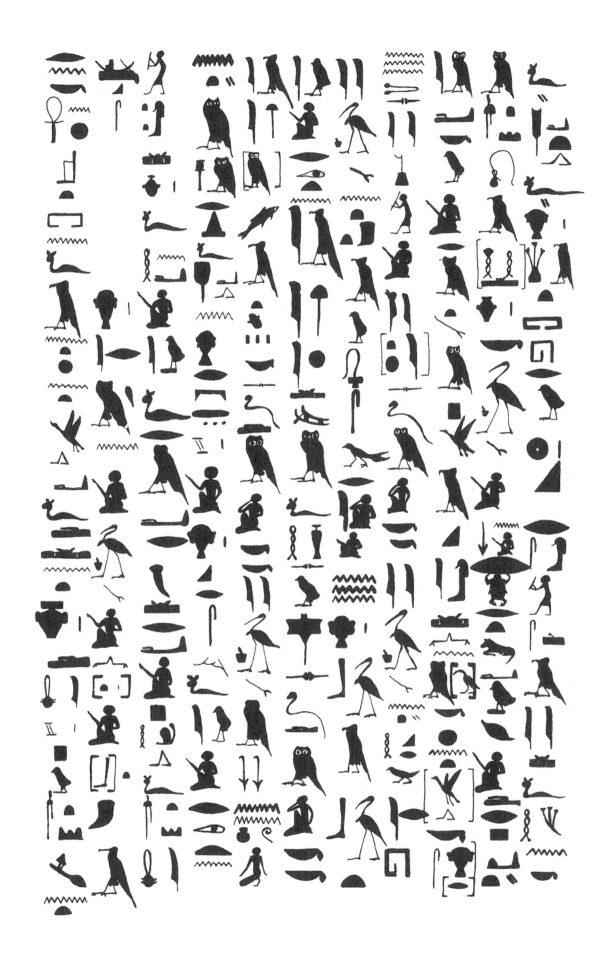

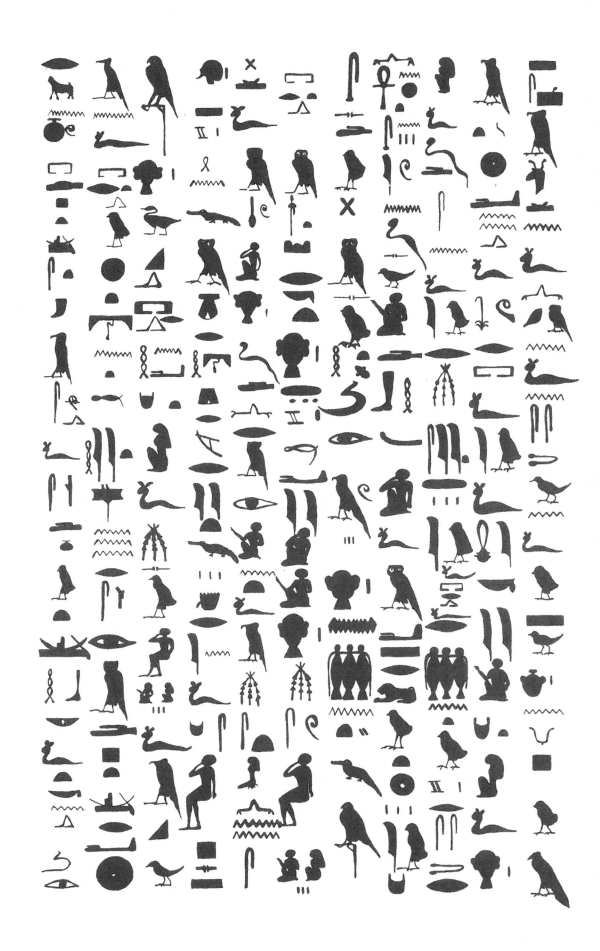

138

139

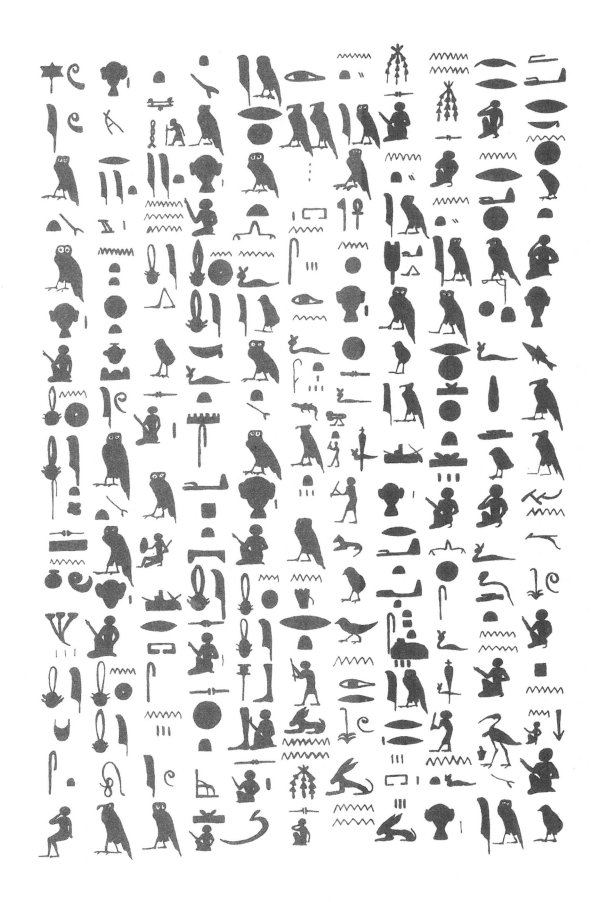

For further reading on the teachings of Ancient Egypt

The Egyptian Miracle
An Introduction to the Wisdom of the Temple
R.A. Schwaller de Lubicz • Illustrated by Lucie Lamy
ISBN 0-89281-008-4 • $18.95 paperback

The Egyptian Miracle is an indispensable guide to the transcendental science expressed by the architecture, the texts, and the proportions of the Ancient Egyptian temple. Introducing the High Science of Egypt and of Pythagoras, de Lubicz discusses measure and how it relates to man, to the esoteric significance of number, and to the geometric elements. He also offers insights into the physics of alchemy, the nature of color and sound, and the esoteric structure of the planetary system, concluding with essential philosophical texts and initiatic teachings from his masterwork, *The Temple of Man*.

The Opening of the Way
A Practical Guide to the Wisdom Teachings of Ancient Egypt
Isha Schwaller de Lubicz • 0-89281-572-8 • $14.95 paperback

This guidebook to the teachings of ancient Egypt is based on the spiritual principles that were the foundation of both the Egyptian Temple and other Western esoteric traditions. These principles reveal to us a higher intelligence, known to the ancient Egyptians as the "intelligence of the heart."
The Opening of the Way provides specific tools for comprehension and application of the ancient esoteric teachings. The author shows the relation of the body systems to sources of vital energy, giving us a key to self-mastery and a connection with higher consciousness.

Journey into the Light
The Three Principles of Man's Awakening
Isha Schwaller de Lubicz • 0-89281-038-6 • $14.95 paperback

A companion volume to the author's *Opening of the Way*, this text, in the form of a novel, portrays the transformative encounter of the modern, scientific, and rational mentality with the suprarational, spiritual intelligence that guides us on the Path of the Mysteries. With scholarship and deep insight the author traces the root of knowledge through Buddhism, Hinduism, and Christianity all the way back to the sacred science of Egypt. In so doing she enables us to discover the symbolism and rites that are the bridge to the spiritual life.

Hathor Rising
The Power of the Goddess in Ancient Egypt
Alison Roberts, Ph.D. • 0-89281-621-X • $16.95 paperback
183 black and white illustrations

Drawing from temple art, myths, rituals, and poetry, *Hathor Rising* is the first book to seriously examine the feminine aspect of the complex Egyptian pantheon. The book sheds new light on the important role of the fiery goddess Hathor Sekhmet, whose importance was emphasized by the serpent emblem coiled over the forehead of every Pharaoh—the supreme symbol of royalty and power. In this important book Dr. Roberts provides a powerful new perspective on women's theology.

Temple of the Cosmos

The Ancient Egyptian Experience of the Cosmos

Jeremy Naydler

0-89281-555-8 • $19.95 paperback • 164 black and white illustrations

Oxford scholar Jeremy Naydler explores Egypt's sacred geography and mythology, revealing an ancient consciousness in tune with the rhythms of the earth.

"A valuable and original work." **John Anthony West**
Author of *The Serpent in the Sky*

"An ambitious and lucid interpretation of ancient Egyptian consciousness, especially with respect to the experience of the sacred. As such the book also sheds light on the wild and mysterious psychospiritual currents of our present time, including the Goddess re-emergence." **Robert Masters, Ph.D.**
Author of *The Goddess Sekhmet*

Her-Bak

The Living Face of Ancient Egypt

Isha Schwaller de Lubicz • 0-89281-003-3 • $16.95 paperback

This vivid re-creation of the spiritual life of ancient Egypt is seen through the eyes of young Her-Bak, candidate for initiation into the sublime mysteries of the Temple. This fictional account, a companion volume to Her-Bak: Egyptian Initiate, traces his development through the stages of his spiritual ascent, from the lessons Nature teaches him as a young boy, his education as a scribe, and finally as a candidate for service in the Temple. Isha Schwaller de Lubicz based her account on years of research at the temples of Luxor and Karnak.

Her-Bak

Egyptian Initiate

Isha Schwaller de Lubicz • 0-89281-002-5 • $16.95 paperback

This second and independent volume continues Her-Bak's spiritual quest, as he is initiated into the Inner Temple and follows his progressive penetration of the esoteric aspects of the Egyptian Mystery teachings, showing the evolution of one individual's life through the phases of temple training. The Her-Bak stories are set between the Twentieth and Twenty-first Dynasties, at Karnak in the Valley of the Kings.

These and other Inner Traditions titles are available at many fine bookstores or, to order directly from the publisher, send a check or money order for the total amount, payable to Inner Traditions, plus $3.00 shipping and handling for the first book and $1.00 for each additional book to:

Inner Traditions, P.O. Box 388, Rochester, VT 05767